# Servant Leadership in Management Practice

# Servant Leadership in Management Practice:

## *Welcome to the Foodbank*

By

Suzanne Kane

**Cambridge
Scholars**
Publishing

Servant Leadership in Management Practice: Welcome to the Foodbank

By Suzanne Kane

This book first published 2020

Cambridge Scholars Publishing

Lady Stephenson Library, Newcastle upon Tyne, NE6 2PA, UK

British Library Cataloguing in Publication Data
A catalogue record for this book is available from the British Library

ISBN (10): 1-5275-6036-8
ISBN (13): 978-1-5275-6036-9

# CONTENTS

# ACKNOWLEDGEMENTS

The original idea for foodbank research was supported by Salford Business School's Pump Priming initiative in 2015. The research later developed a separate, but particularly important focus on servant leadership which is represented here.

My grateful thanks go to Mr Andrew Mackenzie for his friendship, sympathetic reading of the text, and informed guidance.

I also wish to thank Archbishop Doye Agama for supporting access to relevant parties and helpful discussions towards the development of this research.

It is essential to highlight the vital contribution from the interviewees who kindly engaged in this research. They are anonymous here, but my gratitude is offered to them for their significant ongoing contribution to society and for the sharing of their candid and valuable narratives. The story of this research belongs to them and their communities, long may they triumph over adversity.

Dr Suzanne Kane

# ORGANISATION OF THIS BOOK

The starting point for this book is a review of servant leadership and how many well-known authors have situated their view of this subject. It situates this concept in the context of foodbanks and the volunteer workforce, bringing together the personal narratives of individual volunteers. The issues which emerged from these stories are presented in reference to volunteering, supportive management, organisation, and reflections on the future of volunteer community groups.

The book also offers an explanation of the narrative approach utilised to record the personal stories of those involved, highlighting specific dominant themes in the narratives, which are framed with quotations to heighten understanding and meaning within the commentary. Reflection and discussion on the main points illuminate the detailed narratives, and underline the importance of the unpaid workforce. The conclusion includes some practical concerns, which will impact upon the future of the foodbank emergency food service, as we know it today.

## Chapter 1: Introduction

Introduction and overview of the book.

## Chapter 2: Literature-The case for servant leadership

Many well-known authors have written on the theoretical, philosophical, and practical aspects of servant leadership. This chapter reviews the main themes within these explanations and explores links with aspects of volunteering and the foodbank context.

## Chapter 3: Literature-The context of foodbanks and volunteers

Literature of an academic, government and research nature is reviewed in this chapter. Also, there is a specific section showing that the geographical location is significant to the context of the investigation. The nature of the related themes between foodbanks and volunteering is considered.

## Chapter 4: Place and the narrative approach

This chapter sets the scene of the foodbank environment and presents an overview of the questionnaire information provided by volunteers who participated in the investigation. There is an explanation of the narrative approach used here to record the personal stories of those involved.

## Chapter 5: The narratives

This chapter represents the content of the narratives. Specific dominant themes are suggested and the main points from the narratives are stated with quotations employed to heighten understanding and meaning within the commentary.

## Chapter 6: The outlier

Presented in this chapter is a contrary narrative to that which was set by the prior presentation of common stories expressed by the majority. This narrative stands in stark contrast to the mostly faith-based support groups and appears to be the exception. Again, the main points from the narratives are highlighted with quotations employed to heighten understanding and meaning of the commentary.

## Chapter 7: Conclusion, discussion and comments

This chapter provides reflection and discussion on the main points illuminated by the detailed narratives. The importance of the unpaid workforce and appropriate supportive management is underlined. This section concludes with some practical concerns, which will impact upon the future of the foodbank emergency food service as we know it today.

# CHAPTER 1

# INTRODUCTION

Almost fifty years ago Robert Greenleaf employed the term "servant leadership" to promote an enduring concept, which spoke of a servant leader who is servant first and leader second. The primary impulse is that of service to others which calls upon leadership qualities. As such, leadership is a supporting aspect, while service is the driving force. Servant leaders cannot simply lead those that serve, they must themselves continue to serve. Leadership should not be the dominant factor, leadership power which corrupts and causes conflict for some must be tempered with the notion of service. Greenleaf suggested checks and balances including questions to measure the concept of servant leadership in practice. These included:

"Do those served grow as persons?

Do they, while being served, become healthier, wiser, freer, more autonomous, more likely themselves to become servants?

And, what is the effect on the least privileged in society?

Will they benefit or at least not be further deprived?" (Greenleaf Centre for Servant Leadership 2018)

The stated tenets in Greenleaf's explanation elegantly relate to the purpose of this book, which is to present the significance of supportive management practices portrayed in the narratives of those who are managed through a servant leadership approach. That is, not to say that the managers in this context are describing themselves as servant leaders. On the contrary, it is in the views of those who are managed and use descriptions which support defined aspects of the servant leadership approach. Due consideration will be given to the most appreciated components of such support and how this may be sympathetically introduced elsewhere. The context from which the narratives emerge is that of volunteer workers at UK foodbanks. The collection of narratives from volunteers was enabled through the Biographic Narrative Interpretive Methodology (Wengraf 2001). What emerged are insights into the diverse community of individuals who continue to volunteer, the admiration afforded to those who take on management responsibilities in this context, and how managers continue to inspire long-term commitment from volunteer staff.

The personal stories of the volunteers speak of the reasons why they first chose to make a regular commitment of their own time for no financial recompense. They also speak of their shared experiences and how they envisage the future of their work within foodbanks. Food shortages evoke strong emotions about home, family and survival, to which these narratives attest. Thoughtful insights into this diverse community network and how it is managed are provided through the testaments of the individuals who continue to volunteer at a time when many of our social services are dependent upon the support of charitable projects. This book presents examples of how these projects survive on limited resources and rely on the resourcefulness of dedicated volunteers and managers. The frank and well-informed reflections about the managers suggest appreciation of the management style utilised and appears to be key to how the ongoing, long-term commitment of volunteer staff can be supported into the future. Also, of interest, is the strong argument that communities should remain in control of volunteer services and not defer to government control.

Many of our social services are in crisis and depend upon charitable community projects to support those in dire need. Foodbanks are places of last resort for many vulnerable clients, and the story of these community-based projects is about far more than emergency food rations. Therefore, it would be a tragedy if these services were to disappear due to poor management and leadership of volunteer staff. This small-scale study, of sixteen highly detailed narrative interviews (from six different foodbanks), focuses on volunteers who work to support foodbanks in the North West of England, UK. All but one of the foodbanks in this study were located at premises provided or part-funded by local churches. This is a region that saw the greatest number of service users at foodbanks in the UK and year on year increases in the number of users from 2011 to the present day (Trussell Trust Foodbank Statistics). As this is a region that has seen a continued increase in the number who require support, qualitative details of how these groups endure and assist those in greatest need are of importance to community support planning.

In general, while managers may inform staff of what is expected of them, how they should treat clients, and what is acceptable behaviour, our practice often reflects how we are treated ourselves. Therefore, managers as champions of good behaviour are important in shaping staff values, organisational culture, and morale. All too often we are privy to less than adequate examples of management behaviour. However, this book portrays true narratives about good managers by the people who are willing to be led by them on a long-term basis for no financial remuneration. Welcome to the foodbank.

# CHAPTER 2

## LITERATURE-THE CASE FOR SERVANT LEADERSHIP

The title of this book "Servant leadership in management practice: welcome to the foodbank" documents an obvious premise of believing that servant leadership can be seen in the everyday practices reported here. The narrative elements contained in this book not only illuminate the practical commonplace aspects of volunteering in the foodbank context, but also share the many and varied personal rationales for why individuals first chose to volunteer and why they continue to volunteer. Also, in many cases, there is personal commentary about the genuine gratitude and respect for those who take on the management roles which give professional support and guidance to many foodbank community projects. But we also see that many of those who consider themselves to be simply providing a service are actually doing so much more and holding many forms of responsibility. As such, the thoughtful and richly detailed individual stories contribute to our overall understanding of what it is to volunteer and additionally the importance of dedicated managers who willingly accept the difficult questions and the testing circumstances that may occur, which go way beyond what might be expected of a normal volunteering experience. Even above and beyond this are those irregular times of conflict or misunderstandings between service users and service providers. However, these are few and far between and the managers who may or may not hold an official title are always onsite or easily contactable and do much of the invisible work that often remains unrecognised, but noted by the valuable volunteers who take up the daily routines which require such background work in support of what they do for service users. The work which goes on behind the scenes may be to secure small funding pots to prop up parts of the service, or there may be meetings and informal conversations to build an external network of further support in the foodbank service. The time spent getting positive messages out to the local community and beyond is not insignificant and all part of the veiled multitude of activities that continue after opening hours. However, the dedication to also be front of house does not go unnoticed and continues to be uppermost in everyone's mind when the foodbank doors are open. Yet, importantly, the managers allow each volunteer their own responsibilities while continuing to support actions that require further guidance. The managers do not forget their commitment to the volunteers as individuals, as well as to the foodbank as a service. It is of little wonder then that these managers are thus admired and valued and surely candidates for inclusion in the category of servant leader. But as Breslin (2017, 1) keenly makes note:

> *"Within the concept of servant leadership, volunteers are not simply followers but are leaders in their own right. As such, they display both follower and leadership characteristics."*

We see this in the stories from foodbank volunteers, they are all happy to work out of sight while completing administrative duties, sorting goods, stocking the storeroom, and preparing tea, coffee or cold drinks for the service users. Some would prefer to remain out of the public eye, but when required to be in public they readily do so and engage in management of the front desk, admissions, checking eligibility of service users, discussing the contents of food packages and the options which may be available that day. They are also always available to sit with service users, perhaps share a cup of tea and talk, in the hope that they may make the process somewhat less uncomfortable and whenever possible to suggest additional contacts or services that may be of further help.

To consider the potentiality of links to servant leadership from the narrative accounts, we must begin with Robert Greenleaf and his use of the term "servant leadership", which is a concept that has caught the imagination of many who would wish to promote a supportive style of leadership and management. There are two particular terms here in want of further explanation, firstly the servant leader concept, which is central to Greenleaf's approach, but also the importance of followers who are required to balance this conundrum and allow it to work in practice.

## Servant leadership

Servant leadership promotes servant or stewardship as the most important facet to pass on to each generation of leaders and managers. Leading those that choose to serve is important and engagement in serving is an individual choice for leaders and followers. Those providing leadership must also serve on equal terms. On many occasions, this may require getting one's hands dirty and this willingness must remain a constant as this involvement at the coalface is a powerful reminder of why any individual is working within a particular environment (a reminder of their initial core commitments). Equally though is the presence of mind to know when to allow others to take on responsibilities which they may or may not actually seek to do. Sadly, the power of leadership has been known to corrupt, which is why the notion of service has relevance and binds us to recognising the value of others in its purest sense. Veeder (2011) makes particular note that:

> "...servant leadership has become popular in the world of leadership studies in the last thirty years in part as a response to the negative effects of improper use of power. This power being wielded through phenomena such as: industrialisation, globalisation, and various other-isms, which have often widened the gap between the leader and the led, the haves and the have-nots, and men and women".

The foundational idea of bringing servant and leader together as embodied as one and by each individual (at least in potential) and proposing that they, in their ideal state, are part of the whole, is that which envelopes the concept. It also sheds some light on placing other considered opposites together such as "haves and have-nots" and promotes evaluation of overall value of each state in society. A realisation comes forth that when taking different perspectives we can all be viewed as belonging to each category and it is only the human and sometimes inhuman use of measurement that often suggests such as "have-nots" also means of no value.

Reports of corruption and suffering due to inappropriate, unethical, and sometimes illegal activity damages all levels of trust. While inclusive actions and trust in others may sometimes appear to be difficult, and may create conflict within our own plans, concerns and thinking, the intention of service must continue to live within the concept of servant leadership. Such difficulties underline the importance of the factors of supporting others to grow as individuals, for the individual's sake, providing care and attention while, at the same time, encouraging others to act as servants and be effective in assisting those in need are all tenets endorsed by the Greenleaf Centre for Servant Leadership (2018).

Prior note is made of the links that have been highlighted on many occasions between leadership and corruption, and interestingly, Laub (2018, 77) promotes that:

> "Servant leadership is the only leadership approach that recognises the danger of leader self-interest and counters that self-interest with a clear other focus directed toward the followers, to those led. The focus of the servant leader on those led is a critical point that distinguishes this approach from somewhat similar approaches like Transformational Leadership".

As it is of no sense at all to hope that negative or destructive thoughts will be banished from the minds of all who choose that path of accepting servant leadership, the focal point of others as of paramount importance is the linchpin that acts as an integral guide to that which is truly of significance and shines a light into the dark corners of destructive practice as harmful to both leaders and followers alike. That is not to say that it can ever be considered to be an easy path. It is likely that servant leaders must find some comfort in the practice of being of great worth, which may not be an identity that we inhabit easily in the twenty-first century environment. Being a celebrity for no good reason, having fame for ambitions that do no good, portraying skills in belittling others and working in support of no-one but oneself, all appear to be revered in our media culture. When it is uncovered that these, so-called, personalities are sneaking around and secretly doing good and kind works, we are always taken aback. It suggests that they felt they could not find fame unless they were infamous in our modern-day world. This proposes the odd thesis that only the brave can do good and be open and honest in doing so, for they attract the possibility of being greatly reviled! It appears that goodness is all very well so long as it is decidedly well-hidden and no-one is acknowledged. Few of us are immune to such a disposition and it chimes closely with the idea in servant leadership that the good work of the leader must not step away from the essence of the servant. So, while we may find the stories of sinners more interesting than that of saints, in times of distress we would all wish that any hand of friendship came from the goodness in the heart of an individual.

While servant leadership supports all that is good about serving others, it should not be held up as a paragon that will solve all issues of inappropriate management and leadership practice. It would be unfair to expect a cure-all concept, but it is also much more than a set of principled statements to uphold ethical practice, it is an invitation for each individual to understand why they believe and behave as they do. Peter Senge (cited in Frick 2004) specifically makes note:

*"...I think it is a mistake for people to look to 'servant leadership' as a kind of formulaic solution... For above all, Robert Greenleaf's writings were*

*concerned with what motivates us and how we might cultivate deeper sources of motivation".*

In addition to this, Frick (2004) also comments that:

*"There is no master plan for living as a servant-leader, but it certainly involves learning from those who have tried valiantly to do so in their personal and organisational lives, as Robert K. Greenleaf did".*

The notion of people who have previously committed themselves to work as servant leaders, and those who presently do so without such a notion or title, help us all to understand how this may be done and the potential for development within us all. You may imagine that finding such leadership potential in all of us is too much to ask. However, the concept of servant leadership would counter this argument by considering that those who believe themselves not to be natural candidates or rightful successors, may actually embody more potential than those who seek out servant leadership for themselves. It is a conundrum indeed.

Narratives are particularly important here as they carry the stories which underpin our understanding and ignite the desire to both replicate and go beyond that which is observed. Servant-leadership is not promoted as a specifically documented doctrine or theory. Much of the approach is designed to encourage our own understanding of ourselves and how this may help us to help others. However, as noted in A Servant Leadership Primer (Frick 2004), the main points can be seen to include: holding a personal notion of being a servant ahead of being a leader, practicing good listening skills, using power in an ethical manner and preferably by persuasion, seeking group consensus, developing and utilising foresight, withdrawing to seek wisdom and recognise intuition. Alongside these are the recognition of acceptance and empathy, conceptualising, and nurturing community. None of these points can explain the whole, nor is the whole complete, just as human life it is a continuous work in progress. The aim here being to continually progress rather than not, and the progress seen as important and precious is not for the few but for all individuals. The benefits are for each to be supported and for that support to be repeated by each individual for another (thus every domino feels the impact of the unbroken chain). This is a simple concept of enormous relevance for contentment in each of us which in time and given ample opportunity may love company as much as misery is said so to do. Much has been said here of servant leadership as a concept but each leadership is in want of followers, so the art of interpretation now falls on this term. Liden, Wayne, Zhao and Henderson (2008, 162) provide the segue:

*"Servant leadership is based on the premise that to bring out the best in their followers, leaders rely on one-to-one communication to understand the abilities, needs, desires, goals, and potential of those individuals. With knowledge of each follower's unique characteristics and interests, leaders then assist followers in achieving their potential...because followers are nested within leaders, servant leadership may exhibit both between-leader and within-leader variation with respect to outcomes. We contend that the relationships that form between leaders and followers are central to servant leadership".*

## Followership

The act of leadership exalts the potential for followers and in Robert Greenleaf's words (reproduced in the 25th Anniversary Edition of his work

– A Journey into the Nature of Legitimate Power and Greatness, 2002, p256) he details that:

> "Followership is an equally responsible role [as leadership] because it means that the individual must take the risk to empower the leader and to say, in the matter at hand, 'I will trust your insight'. Followership implies another preparation in order that trusting, empowering the leader, will be a strength-giving element…".

Schwarz, Newman, Cooper and Eva (2016, 1026) repeat the words of Robert Greenleaf, when they note that:

> "Followers in turn view the servant leader as a role model and mirror his or her behaviours, thus becoming servant leaders themselves".

The meaning here is that servant leaders are seen to support followers, as best they can, in the development of their own individual chosen ways to progress. Followers then replicate this service for others, thus enacting servant leadership themselves. This can be said to have its foundation in such actions as:

> "a servant leader will listen to and understand the aspirations of his or her followers and will mentor followers to achieve these goal". (Schwarz, Newman, Cooper & Eva 2016, 1026).

The more explanation that is given to distinguish servant leaders from followers, seems to have the opposite influence. The examination serves to bring them closer together, as Horsman (2018, 63) makes note:

> "The need to authentically influence and persuade rather than command and control denotes a fundamental value shift that provides insight into the

*kind of humble respect and self-examination leaders and followers need to*
*undergo... A need for leadership development that no longer distinguishes*
*leaders from followers as superiors and subordinates, but rather assumes*
*that we are all leaders and followers".*

The heartfelt narratives of everyday service contained in this book include
a number of descriptions which portray recognised elements of the servant
leadership approach. Such supportive management and leadership
behaviours are evidently of great and deep importance to those followers,
also known as volunteers, working within the foodbank context, caring for
others, giving their time and expertise, providing a vital service which could
not survive without them. The receivers of the service are grateful for the
work of the volunteers, the volunteers have naught but praise for the
commitment of those acting as managers and leaders in the foodbank, and
those continuing to manage the volunteers can be seen to care for each as
individuals. This presents the ongoing story of servant leadership in the
foodbank. The proof of the story is seen in the continuous practice of
service to others. Many authors have written in regard to servant
leadership from different perspectives, some of which are considered in
this section. To begin, Parris and Peachey (2013) suggest servant
leadership as:

*"A new research area linked to ethics, virtues, and morality".*

This is important as it shows how a concept can be recognised at different
times from different perspectives. Ethical practice is certainly an area that
is highly relevant to the servant leadership approach. However, Robert
Greenleaf's work began much earlier than this and takes us back to his first

published essay in 1970 (Centre for Servant Leadership 2019): Words from Greenleaf's 25th Anniversary Edition of Servant Leadership (2002, 21) include:

> *"the great leader is seen as servant first, and that simple fact is the key to his greatness".*

A person can be leading all the time but act as servant first because *"deep down inside"* that is what they are, to serve others being that which is most important to them. This simple, but refined statement of Greenleaf's concept goes straight to the heart of the issue and leaves us with no doubt that the best of all leadership is that of service to others as individuals. Although the practice of such is unlikely to be described as easy by anyone engaged in such service, the achievement is great and there is opportunity for the cycle to continue into the lives of others, if only the goodness of the action could become infectious and addictive.

## Servant leadership –philosophy, theory and practice

Crowther (2018, 1) writes about the foundations of servant leadership theory and notes that:

> *"The ideas and concepts for servant leadership have been around for centuries in different forms. Even when Aristotle and later Aquinas discussed leadership, they pondered the concepts of virtues as an important component of human life and leadership. Other philosophers such as Plato discussed leadership but with some different ideas that became mainstream ideas for ruling and power".*

Crowther goes on to explain:

Chapter 2

*"This focus on power carried the day in leadership thinking with concepts of leadership like in Machiavelli's-The Prince that endorsed a power center to leadership...while in other contexts alternative concepts for leadership became part of the lived experiences of leaders".*

He then relates the beginnings of servant leadership expressing that Greenleaf:

*"believed that there were students who were looking for a better way to lead and there were others as well like trustees...who wanted more effective models for leadership".*

Certainly this is a discussion that relates to conversations had by trustees at foodbanks. They take on great personal responsibilities and need a mechanism which they are able to trust for the purposes of safeguarding their own and their family's financial security.

Robert Greenleaf's work came from a lifetime of experience. Great ideas of many kinds come from our life experiences, but fewer are recorded for posterity. In his retirement, Robert Greenleaf reflected upon his work and life experience and continued the activity of research and engagement in writing about a concept to progress the support of others as the commitment and heart of management and leadership. He wrote of this heart as a living and life-giving essential without which veracity the management and leadership of others simply does not truly exist. Without the heart of a servant leader you may organise, collaborate, engage, and much more. But, without the concept of care for each individual as an individual we are simply moving pieces around a chessboard. These are pieces which may or may not have any impact, just as unconnected, underestimated, and unsupported individuals may do. Talk of wasted resources is evident in many discussions of modern-day life, but there is little as sad as the waste of individual life which could be supported to higher potential. Importantly, Greenleaf does not refer to human beings as resources which is to his great credit, for human potential is so much more. In Spears (1998, 8-9) presentation and discussion of Greenleaf's early work and his considered categorisation of ten characteristics, he particularly expresses philosophical underpinnings in the characteristic of building community. This last of the characteristics states that:

*"The servant-leader senses that much has been lost in recent human history as a result of the shift from local communities to large institutions as the primary shaper of human lives. This awareness causes the servant-leader to seek to identify some means for building community among those who work within a given institution. Servant leadership suggests that true community can be created among those who work in businesses and other institutions. Greenleaf said: 'All that is needed to rebuild community as a viable life form for large numbers of people is for enough servant-leaders to show the way, not by mass movements, but by each servant-leader demonstrating his [or her] own unlimited liability for a quite specific community related group'. These ten characteristics of servant leadership are by no means exhaustive. However, they serve to communicate the power and promise that this concept offers to those who are open to its invitation and challenge...There are a half-dozen major areas in which the principles of servant leadership are being applied in significant ways. The first area has to do with servant leadership as an institutional philosophy and model. Servant leadership crosses all boundaries and is being applied by a wide variety of people working with for-profit businesses, not-for-profit corporations, churches, universities, and foundations."*

Spears panegyric continues Greenleaf's convictions of individual commitment and the importance of community coming together much as the same way as a servant-leader may be misunderstood as an incongruent term. Other authors who speak of philosophical elements in Greenleaf's seminal work include Horsman (2018, 2) as he considers servant leadership within the realms of philosophy, saying:

> "[servant leadership] *is a relatively stable open philosophy in perpetual transformation*".

Lapointe and Vandenberghe (2018) note that:

> "*Greenleaf's early work reflected more a servant leadership philosophy than a servant leadership theory...*"

while Laub (2018, 142) *suggests that:*

> "*Servant leadership is best viewed not as one leadership style among many, but is a mindset, a set of underlying assumptions that guide our leadership philosophy and behaviour*".

This portrays a much more human-centred approach than a resource-centred view.

Continuing this human and humane perspective, Hakanen and Pessi (2018) suggest the importance of compassion in the workplace when saying that:

> "*There is also a theory of leadership approaching the topic in a positive and empowering manner that clearly considers both compassion and co-passion; both how to ease suffering at work and how to build proactive engagement and innovativeness at work, namely, servant leadership.*

*Servant leadership as a philosophy of leadership and a set of practices provides several approaches and tools to lead compassionately and passionately".* Relating this to Greenleaf's idea of servant leadership, they say: *"...when introducing the theory of servant leadership, [Greenleaf] did not explicitly write about compassion and servant leadership. However, he discussed empathy and acceptance as essential parts of being a servant leader. With good reason it can be said that servant leadership is the theory of compassionate leadership".*

In line with this commentary, Kantharia (2012) gives high praise indeed to servant leadership. In a study of leadership styles he denotes that:

*"Servant Leadership seems to cut across all leadership theories and provides foundational philosophy for theories which are congruent with the growth of humankind".*

Frick (2004, 21) states:

*"I consider servant leadership a philosophy rather than a theory of leadership"*

The Encyclopaedia of Management (Hill 2012, 897) professes servant leadership to be

*"a philosophical approach to organizational management that prioritizes practical participation over the oversight responsibilities of the leader in organizational activities. The leader's execution of authority, power, and influence is not as important as his or her direct participation as an ordinary member of the organization's work teams".*

However, specific relationships are also made to theory, linking it to:

*"...the great person theory, path-goal theory, and theory Y"* (Hill 2012, 897).

But, Parris and Peachy (2013, 378) state that Greenleaf himself suggested that the concept of servant leadership portrays *"a way of life"*, they suggest that this did perhaps not chime well with relationships to *"management technique'* and *'slowed the acceptance of this leadership theory in academia".* They also note the extensive work on servant leadership by Larry Spears and highlight that his identification of:

> *"... characteristics of Servant Leaders from Greenleaf's writings: listening, empathy, healing, awareness, persuasion, conceptualization, foresight, stewardship, commitment to the growth of people, and building community".*

In qualifying this, Laub (2018, 115) notes:

> *"...it was Greenleaf who developed the philosophical underpinnings of the concept [of servant leadership] and it was Spears who codified the list of ten characteristics drawn from the work of Greenleaf".*

Ferch (2011, 122) posits that the people, who are considered to be today's thought leaders, uphold the values of such characteristics. She also specifically notes, in relation to the first of Greenleaf's servant leader stated characteristics, that:

> *"...listening occurs both in one-to-one relationships and in the context of a higher order more concerned with the life of the community as a whole...In servant leadership, the listener becomes a person who sees more clearly his or her own faults, works diligently to overcome them, and understands then how to bring healing to others".*

While all the characteristics appear equal in consideration, listening certainly defines the start of this conceptual process and potentially engages more servant leaders of the future. Listening to others gifts the opportunity for the development of empathy and understanding to grow and thus expands the possibility of progress in the support of others who we may never previously have shared our life experiences. In further acknowledgement of the value of listening, Adair (2002, 42) notes:

> "The natural badge of such inner humility towards all things is silence. 'Silence is of the gods', says one Chinese proverb. Again there is a paradox here, for the Greek and Roman traditions exalted the place of oratory in leadership. For Greek leaders who had to persuade their fellow citizens by reason, it was speech that is golden, not silence. Yet listening is important, and it is difficult for a leader to listen if he or she is speaking or waiting to speak. 'No one can safely appear in public unless he himself feels that he would willingly remain in retirement', wrote the medieval Christian writer Thomas a Kempis".

This is a fairly alien concept in modern society. Shouting to be heard is often the order of the day. Quiet souls are questioned as to their ill-health, as if quietness must equate to not being oneself. This idea of quietness being an indicator of sadness, tiredness, illness and worse still, weakness, is a fashionable affectation which seems unable to recognise silence as thoughtful or rejuvenating. The appearance, which may of course be pretence, is a majority of the population getting the best from thinking and sense-making by enacting it out loud. For some, talking and shouting is a coping technique that they adopt to deal with the world. Not giving way or allowing space for others to be part of a discussion can sometimes seem like a modern-day sport or game that some have little interest in, but many must act out. Shouting people down or simply creating more noise than is necessary has become normal. Talking loudly is used as a weapon. There may, of course, be an equal number of people who speak far less, speak quietly, engage in quiet thoughtfulness for the purposes of reflection and careful consideration. For as many people as there are who recharge their batteries by making some kind of noise, there may be just as many who are energised by silence. But importantly, they are not on show, they do not wilfully attract attention. They are not parading, they are still. Perhaps neither preference is a choice, it is simply a natural process. But the noise makers do, of course, have the operational advantage as the quiet ones do not impose upon the volume, but the noise always obliterates the quiet!

Whether naturally quiet or not as an individual, the underlying necessary rule of placing others first is always paramount for servant leadership, as Sumni and Mesner-Andolsek (2017, 120) remind us:

> *"Aristotle's definition of a righteous man who 'does not allocate more assets to oneself than one is proportionally supposed to, and puts efforts into serving and aiding others', we can see the point of contact of the philosophy of servant leadership in the fact that a leader first and foremost takes care of his employees and then himself".*

Sumni and Mesner-Andolsek (2017, 129) also provide a useful bridge in-between philosophy and practical application, when they note that:

> *"...servant leadership is not merely a theoretical concept as it is important for it to be reflected in daily practice".*

Furthermore, is the sentiment of a two-way support system recognised in volunteerism that is supported through servant leadership and as noted by Breslin (2017, 3):

> *"Volunteers can use foresight to help leaders anticipate the future and its consequences through their lived experiences in other situations".*

Over many years, media stories have reported on the range of damaging business deals that have impacted upon customers, employees, our legal systems and our perspectives of commercial business in general. Such reports remain important in informing us of the areas for particular attention when unprofessional, unsatisfactory and illegal actions come to light, which may impact on many more in terms of social and financial implications. Therefore, we are tasked to facilitate investigations in an attempt to prevent repetition. However disturbing it is to hear of unacceptable practice in business, some action may prove to be devastating for both individuals and groups that are in no-way connected to the decision-making processes that have caused catastrophic consequences in countries, regions, communities, families and for individuals alike. Impacts of poor management and leadership decisions can be both dangerous and contemptible. Qiu and Dooley (2019) suggest that:

> *"...given that the rampant misconduct and corruption has led to the interrogation and incarceration of numerous business leaders, servant leadership, with its emphasis on the benefits for the employees and society at large, should be urgently applied...".*

Hill (2012, 897) notes the practical approaches in servant leadership as "collaborative" and individuals are said to accept:

*"...a calling to serve selflessly rather than an opportunity for articulating self-centered interests".*

However, a critique of servant leadership in practice by Liu (2019) suggests that those who consider themselves to be servant leaders may find that colleagues take a different view. This is a relevant point regarding the perspectives of others who are experiencing servant leadership from a line manager. So called "followers" must be receptive to the approach in order to benefit from servant leadership in practice and this may take some time and may not always be accepted. If this is the case difficulties will arise for both parties, but the true servant leader would view this as a requirement for further support and understanding of the follower as more consideration can always be afforded, as support of the individual should be infinite and not time-bound. Commenting upon the servant leader as an individual, Cooper (2015) says:

*"A servant leader seeks to create a culture of service, supporting and helping her followers understand their own higher purpose and use their full potential...".*

Sumi and Mesner-Andolsek (2017, 81) suggest a difference between managers and leaders, saying:

*"...a manager can create an excellent organisational strategy or a plan of work, but they are often not skilled enough to put them into practice and motivate employees to participate. Unlike a manager, a leader dedicates himself to the employees as people through the creation of a vision, creativity, making changes, etc".*

Furthermore, on the part of the individual leader, Irving (2018, chap. 3) pronounces:

> *"...purpose provides leaders with the capacity to transcend self-interest. Although self-interest is a natural human instinct, when infused with a sense of greater purpose or meaning a leader is able to transcend base commitments to self and begin to authentically consider the needs of others".*

Although, conceptually, the terms servant and leader may not appear to be an easy concatenation, Stephenson (2017, 81) provides an explanation for practice:

> *"On its face, the concept of servant leadership appears to be a contradiction in terms. When considered in an absolute sense, it does not seem logical to be simultaneously considered both a servant and a leader; however, in practice, these concepts are not mutually exclusive".*

When discussing the place of servant leadership in the creation of positive organisations, Whittington (2018, 71) states that:

> *"The commitment to an employee-first philosophy is also evidence of altruistic, other-centered motives"*

Also suggested is that:

> *"...this philosophy serves as an enabler for creating a unique culture, as well as providing an explicit others-first orientation".*

Within practice, the art of mindfulness associated with servant leadership is noted by Verdorfer and Arendt (2018) as they say:

*"…we believe that genuine servant leadership qualities can also arise as a 'side effect' of mindfulness practice. It is true that, at the beginning, many leaders may have a somewhat self-centred motivation to engage in mindfulness practice."*

However, they suggest that this leads to a more 'objective view' and '…develop greater humility…'. At this point, if you feel that you are being led down the road to believing that management practice in the form of servant leadership can be a thing of fantasy or dreams, Roberts (2015) challenges all such thought by stating that it is not "soft" nor "martyr" based. He goes on to say that:

*"One cannot be a servant leader and not achieve the mission and discipline the workforce".* He specifically notes that: *"…servant leaders are not martyrs; they actively promote self-care and work-life harmony and balance".*

Interestingly, Roberts also gives consideration to integrity in the workplace and promotes that:

*"There is no question of viewing employees as resources and costs…";* he suggests *"all decisions entail a formal calculus of the consequences for the wellbeing of each employee."*

Also, a mix of practices that include:

*"Management by walking around… Holding office hours…without an appointment… [specifically rewarding] difficult or controversial questions. Providing means for anonymous inputs… [via the] use of ongoing employee attitude surveys, focus groups, entrance, engagement and exit interviews…".*

Finally, and perhaps most importantly:

> *"Linking leadership and management advancement to employees...No manager or leader should be hired or advanced with high levels of employee dissatisfaction".*

With a focus on that which employees see in action within the workplace, there is also a view from Yang et al (2018) that:

> *"Employee skills and competence are enhanced by observing servant leaders demonstrating and disseminating knowledge at work".*

With particular regard for

*"Emotion management in the workplace"*, Lu, Zhang and Jia (2018) write of specific contributions from their work which suggest that practices which include aspects of servant leadership

> *"could encourage employees to trust leaders in terms of both affect and cognition, thus enhancing their willingness to express and manage their true feelings at work".*

Much of the detail here alludes to many elements of management which are difficult for both leaders and followers. For instance, the acceptance of personal responsibility may be a harsh reality that some followers are unwilling to recognise, and also one that is not readily accepted by some leaders. But also, in contrast, managers and leaders may be so accustomed to taking personal responsibility that they may struggle to delegate important duties to those that are willing to accept these in order to progress. This can lead to an environment where servants are never seriously seen as progressing into leadership. Also, rather than nondelegation due to worries that work may not be adequately completed, some managers and leaders live in fear of their colleagues being much more capable than themselves and this kind of inferiority complex leads to micro-management as surveillance, which gives work colleagues no inducement to engage in the progression of their own development. This is one indication of an environment where both leader and follower may be useful servants in each other's progress if only they can accept each other as embodying both servant and leadership qualities. However, those in subservient positions must be able to trust their leaders to accept honest communications which are intended to support. Crowther (2018, 2) suggests a wide scope of acceptance of the servant leader model when he says that it:

> "...has been adopted, discussed and lived by many in several different fields. As this model has moved from theory to practice, there are others who have developed and adapted this model in many different contexts".

While the individual is the primary focus in servant leadership, individuals often require the support of team efforts to achieve certain goals, and research on leading teams by Harju, Schaufeil and Hakanen (2018) suggests that the:

> "...servant leadership style may be specifically suited for driving such behaviors, as it focuses primarily on the good of the individual instead of the organization"

In a cross-over between managers and employees, Whang, Xu and Liu (2017) note that

*"…servant leadership by high-level mangers could cascade downward through the organizational hierarchy to influence frontline employees service performance…"* .

Research by Newman, Schwarz, Cooper and Sendjaya (2017) suggests that

*"…servant leadership primarily exerts its influence on followers at the individual level by facilitating social exchange between them and the leader…findings suggest that because servant leaders put follower's development and interests above those of the organization, followers working under servant leaders develop intense personal bonds marked by shared values, open-ended commitment, mutual trust and concern for the welfare of the other party."*

This may be seen as the beginnings of servant leadership emanating from the follower, thus the cycle of support continues to turn. Adair (2002, 37) also comments on the engagement in the service of others in practice when reviewing the work of great leaders:

*"…Socrates had identified the common element of service in all leadership, by insisting that the core responsibility of leaders is to meet human needs. Xenophon had found that it worked in practice. If you came down from your height – literally in the case of a mounted commander and metaphorically in that of a landowner – and worked among people, this action would inspire willing obedience. The Roman leaders who followed his example and teaching found that the same principle worked for them. Both Greeks and Romans were essentially pragmatists. By the exercise of practical reason, they sought to discover what works in leadership, and to a large measure they did so".*

This is an interesting point as it highlights the difference between leaders who engage with followers strategically for their own purposes, and those servant leaders who truly engage in order to serve each individual's needs in spite of the consequences for themselves. Moreover is the view of servant leadership with regard to gender, as Scicluna-Lehrke and Sowden (2017) suggest that one challenge is:

> *"...bridging the gap between how men and women are perceived as leaders and who is believed to be fit to lead. An initial look at servant leadership poses it as a possible solution to narrow the gender gap for leadership roles".*

## Education (servant leadership for learning, teaching, and education)

In the variety of explanations and experiences presented around servant leadership, there is a propensity to relate points to aspects of learning, for example, followers' perspectives of leaders are said to be impacted by their level of prior education:

> *"...data reveals that the higher a leader's education, the higher the respondent perceives that leader's conceptual skills"* (Sumi & Mesner-Andolsek, 2017, 169).

But servant leadership is also found in other areas of the literature related to education and there is an important link, especially in consideration of bringing theory and practice together through shared understanding. Education may be referred to within the institutional view of schools or colleges but can also relate to learning on the shop floor, a community or training centre environment, a foodbank project or elsewhere. As Covey

(2016, 355) makes note when considering the habits of highly effective people and considering the value of lifelong learning:

> *"...continuing education, continually honing and expanding the mind – is vital mental renewal. Sometimes that involves the external discipline of the classroom or systematized study programs; more often it does not. Proactive people can figure out many ways to educate themselves".*

But also, in consideration of servant leadership related to teachers, Peter Senge (2006, 329) provides the following insights:

> *"A great teacher is someone around whom others learn. Great teachers create space for learning and invite people into that space. By contrast, less masterful teachers focus on what they are teaching and how they are doing it. The spirit of a leader as a grower of people was beautifully articulated by Robert Greenleaf...The best test [of the servant leader] is: Do those served grow as persons? Do they become healthier, wiser, freer, more autonomous, more likely themselves to become servants?".*

Laub (2018, 37) suggests that this best test is:

> *"The closest Greenleaf came to defining his concept, though it is not technically a definition".*

Senge (2006, 256), when writing about the development of learning organisations, also promotes the importance of being allowed to learn through experimentation, suggesting the relevance of *"the basic metaphor of prototypes"* and warns that:

> *"Benchmarking and studying best practice will not suffice – because the prototyping process does not involve just incremental changes in*

*established ways of doing things, but radical new ideas and practices that together create a new way of managing".*

In regard of management education and the development of leaders, a striking note of human frailty is illuminated by Roberts (2015) when he suggests:

*"In most leadership development efforts, the preponderance of the focus is on the negative influence of poor character in subordinates. This is consistent with the ubiquitous human proclivity to focus on the character weaknesses of others and avoid the painful self-analysis and introspection of addressing our personal character flaws".*

In regard to research of servant leadership in schools, Nsiah and Walker (2013, 55) suggest that:

*"...it is not enough to talk intellectually about the characteristics of leadership since students and the school community needed to see and feel these characteristics in everyday practice and be guided towards the importance of service in their communities".*

They also make note of the consideration of servant leadership in action as:

*"Positive outcomes inspire people to action. This is what happened with principals who were heartened by positive results such as collaboration, community building, care for one another, and growth in their staff members and students".*

In relation to educational institutions, Nichols (2010, 3) notes Greenleaf's view that:

*"optimal performance [should not be] measured by gains on standardized test or reproducing memorized knowledge."*

Again, this suggests the importance of practice and of education professionals. Nichols (2010, 26) proposes that:

*"Traditionally, the education profession has attracted people who do not seek a great deal of power and who hold a view – at least in a minor capacity – of service to others, namely students".*

Part of this service to students is outlined as giving decision-making powers to the students themselves:

*"...by allowing them some of the decision-making power, it gives them more control over their education, makes evaluation less punitive, and provides an important learning experience by engaging students in the decision-making process"* (Nichols, 2010, 42).

However, it does not seem that there is much in the way of proclamation when it comes to servant leadership in education or anywhere else. This may be for a number of reasons but, Wheeler (2012) in his research of Servant Leadership for Higher Education, makes specific note that people did not seem to want to declare themselves as servant leaders, due to the following:

*"(1) they don't understand the concept well enough and so are uncomfortable being described as a servant leader; (2) they don't want to be put in any 'leadership box' that may limit their flexibility (in their mind being a servant leader suggests you must respond in a particular manner or have a particular set of techniques); (3) these leaders tend to be eclectic, picking ideas and practices from whatever philosophy or theory fits their*

*needs and personality; (4) they may have a sense that servant leadership is too religious or faith-based: (5) they don't like the term servant, which to them implies subservient (I have particularly heard that from people who felt oppressed in the past; and (6) they felt that leadership expectations are too high – something unobtainable".*

Some of the points given here may seem a little out of kilter when referring back to Greenleaf's original foray into the explanation of servant leadership, which promotes all that is good about being a servant first and always remaining so in one's heart and mind. In fact, straying from such a mindset would suggest that you were in danger of leaving servant leadership behind. However, there is so much more in the practice in context and understanding of individual support that it cannot be denied that servant leaders are very likely to be an eclectic mix. But Wheeler (2012) also clearly notes the factor of service in oneself and others when professing:

*"Servants know that getting things accomplished is achieved through others so their task is to find ways to make it happen".*

This specifically underlines the notion of some form of delegation as key in the work and development of servant leadership. It also provides a timely reminder that service is a two-way negotiation which cannot stand alone, servant leadership must commune or perhaps needs community to work effectively.

Speaking of the importance of community in the context of education and servant leadership necessitates the mention of service learning and how this connects with the development of servant leadership in education.

Veeder (2011) provides a very informative piece on this and Harkins, Kozak, and Ray (2018) give clear points regarding this concept. They note that:

*"Service-learning is a complex pedagogical and philosophical tool involving numerous stakeholders, including students, faculty, university administrators and community partners to support student learning and civic engagement, community development and university community collaborations".*

They also inform us that:

*"Universities and faculty incorporate service-learning into institutional and departmental curricula for many reasons including: to meet university goals and to align with civic missions; to facilitate student growth and development; and to share university resources with surrounding communities".*

Importantly, they continue to remind the reader that benefits such as these, simply *"graze the surface"* of the service-learning pedagogical approach, but servant leadership is not specifically noted within the concept. However, servant leadership can be said to call out to all notions of service and as such promotes aspects that are of relevance for engagement on some levels and potentially to share similar or at least compatible goals.

## Servant leadership and the third sector

Finally, in this section, there is need of some commentary about leadership and the third sector (as considered to be voluntary organisations, social enterprises, co-operatives and community groups, not-for-profit organisations and foundationally those organisations which put social impact at the top of their purpose and mission). Unfortunately, recent media reports inform us that some large charitable organisations have been left wanting when elements of corrupt personal behaviour have been brought to light. This has enormous impact upon the way such organisations are perceived by the public, this highlights that no one person should be above guidance and scrutiny of their work, and promotes the importance of service where servant leaders can never be allowed to forget that they are working as the servants of others and should place the wellbeing of others at the heart of everything they do. In the words of Robert Greenleaf:

> *"Do those served grow as persons? Do they become healthier, wiser, freer, more autonomous, more likely themselves to become servants?"*.

Corrupt and corrosive actions do not aid the meeting of such important goals!

The UK Charity Commission reported that charities continue to be relatively well-perceived, but don't like the specific behaviours of some, sadly it is noted that:

> *"...public trust in charities has fallen to the lowest level since 2005."* (Third Sector 2018)

This kind of public response shows how important trust is in the public understanding of the third sector. There is a historical belief, and expectation, that charitable organisations are built on the concept of service to others, which maps appropriately with the idea of servant leadership, but this must be seen in action and be shown to be part of the fabric of such organisations. If they are not in existence to do good, to assist and support others, indeed to serve, then what is their purpose? Commercial organisations are tasked with a certain level of behaviour towards internal and external stakeholders, but nowhere is it more clear than in the third sector that service to others should be upheld as a deep-seated and fixed standard. While members of the public would be perhaps annoyed and/or disillusioned in hearing about inappropriate behaviour in business, this is nothing to the disgust that is felt when those in power within third sector organisations abuse and corrupt their positions, and they do so at the peril of the organisations' wellbeing and the loss of respect from their dutiful and committed colleagues. As important as this partial loss of trust, from the public, for third sector organisations undoubtedly is, recent research from the Institute for Leadership and Management (2019) tells us that at least line managers are:

> *"...most trusted in the third sector compared to line managers in private and public sectors".*

But, they also note that across all sectors the trust in Chief Executive Officers (CEOs) has dropped and the third sector has seen the most significant decrease in trust of their CEOs. While we are all aware and grateful for the valuable service which occurs in all charitable organisations, the good opinion of the public and all stakeholders is vital. A servant leadership approach is surely paramount in such contexts.

## Conclusion

The thoughtful and considered writings of Robert Greenleaf, those supporters of his who worked alongside him, and those who came later to his conceptual approach, provide a view into the possibilities of servant leadership for many contexts. Servant leadership holds up high standards and requires the best of all those engaged with it. Followers are a necessary component, but followers themselves must be, or possibly be in the state of becoming servant leaders, not leaders, never just leaders, but always servant leaders. Greenleaf's ideals are high and there is no easy path, nor is there any end to the path, the commitment to continuing servant leadership does not have an end point, most particularly because these are ideals which must be passed on for others to enact, too.

Questioning ourselves about taking the right or appropriate path and making choices that serve others above ourselves, tends to be seen as denying oneself in order to favour others. It could be viewed as missing out on rewards so that others may reap the benefits of your hard work. But what greater benefit than the satisfaction of continuing along a way that we can recognise as achievement through others and for the good of all? We are part of the all and we benefit as both individuals and communities of practice.

There is a perilous idea in humanity that we can be happy without companionship, that we can be immune from inhumanity in society which harms others, but does not touch us. But, of course, it does touch us and hurts us deeply, the most grievous danger to each individual is in the denial of this, because we cannot hide from that which we know to be true and the memories remain.

# CHAPTER 3

# LITERATURE-THE CONTEXT OF FOODBANKS AND VOLUNTEERS

Literature written around the context of a subject allows consideration of change and progress, or lack of it. For this purpose, the following chapter reviews the specific literature in areas such as Foodbanks, Models and Historical Growth. This provides a review of terms and models of delivery alongside points of historical development. The UK government and Trussell Trust section includes literature commissioned by government departments and the highly significant contribution of the Trussell Trust Foodbank network. The Research and Charities section shows how poverty related to foodbank use goes across the age range from young children to the elderly and all those in between. UK, the North West and Manchester is the section which places further information in the context of foodbanks in the North West of England region. The Individual volunteers section speaks of definitions, day to day responsibilities carried out by the body of unpaid staff, and the demands which are placed upon the service and volunteers who want to deliver even more than is already made available.

## Foodbanks, models and historical growth

There are a number of different ways in which communities attempt to support those in social need and for food provision these come in many forms, which include cooked meals in a cafeteria-style environment, takeaway food via street deliveries and packaged emergency food aid from established foodbank services. Lambie-Mumford (2013) notes:

> *"The Trussell Trust Foodbank Network is a network of community-run (Foodbank) franchises managed by the Trussell Trust, a Christian social action charity. The Foodbank model is designed to be an emergency intervention, providing food for people in the short-term while they await support from other services".*

Bull & Harries (2013) show how the term "foodbank" has covered a diverse range of localised organisations, all networking to alleviate hunger and poverty.

> *"Food banks operate within a spectrum of organisations that exist to help those without enough food to subsist. From soup kitchens through to organisations that campaign for a living wage, there are a great number of charities working to tackle food poverty".*

They note personal contributions of time, skills and other resources in UK foodbanks and comments on the lack of definition specifically attributed to food poverty.

> *"Unlike fuel poverty, there is no official definition of food poverty in the UK, so we cannot be sure of the number of people that are affected. A recent report by Kellogg's defines households that have to spend more than 10% of their income on food as being in food poverty, putting the number of*

*people affected in the UK at roughly 4.7 million...Broadly, food poverty refers to a situation in which, through a combination of rising food prices, stagnating incomes and stricter benefit restrictions, people find themselves unable to afford adequate food to survive"* (Bull & Harries 2013).

Additionally, they suggest the differences which stands in contrast with the highly developed corporate patterns seen in foodbanks in the USA. The modern foodbank movement is traced to the 1960s in Phoenix, Arizona, USA, and the work of retired businessman John Van Hengel. His idea of collecting surplus food from various organisations and storing it in a warehouse for distribution to the needy, spread across the USA in the 1970s. Between 1976 and 1982 the foodbank program in the USA received federal funding and was helped by the US Tax Reform Act of 1976, which encouraged organisations to give to foodbanks at that time. The US foodbanks became more regulated with standardisation of quality control in various areas of their operations. By 1982, federal funding had been discontinued, however, the non-profit organisation America's Second Harvest (also now known as Feeding America) increased its pursuit of alternative sources of financial support. The organisation continued to grow as the practice of "foodbanking" gained acceptance and support from the food industry and local social service providers. Feeding America, as a national chain of foodbanks, now reaches 25 million Americans annually (Second Harvest Foodbank 2019). By 1984 the concept of modern foodbanks in both America and Canada was being utilised in France and Belgium. The Federation of European Foodbanks was launched in 1986 and other European countries joined and continue to do so (European Food Banks Federation 2019).

In contrast to the long-term history of foodbank operations in the USA, foodbanks in the United Kingdom are relatively recent, Lambie-Mumford (2013) notes that:

> *"The first Foodbank was set up by the Trussell Trust in 2000 in Salisbury where they are based. In 2004, the decision was taken by the Trust to develop a way of sharing the model more widely and Foodbank was developed into a not-for-profit 'social' franchise'.*

But there has been a huge rise in the number of welfare projects that are run by volunteer organisations, many of which are faith groups. An obvious example of the level of need and support here are the number of foodbanks increasingly accessed by people in local communities (Downing, Kennedy & Fell 2014, 3). Foodbanks are a response to the income vulnerabilities in parts of the population:

> *'nearly 60 million people turn annually to food banks in 'rich' nations – that is, a level similar to the entire population of France or Italy and representing about 7.2 per cent of the HIC [High income countries] population. Such level could be considered a conservative estimate".* (Gentilini, 2013, 3).

When linked together the need for emergency food support from foodbanks alongside street deliveries of takeaway food and soup kitchen-style cafeterias, denotes a much bigger picture of food insecurity which still does not include conventional food support from social services such as free school meals and the meals at home service (also known as meals on wheels). However, each of these factors is a piece of a much larger jigsaw, which suggests the hidden and creeping scope of food insecurity. Food insecurity in the UK has no single accepted definition which only increases its concealment. One very useful definition of food insecurity as a term is:

> *"Limited or uncertain availability of nutritionally adequate and safe foods or limited or uncertain ability to acquire acceptable foods in socially acceptable ways (e.g. without resorting to emergency food supplies, scavenging, stealing or other coping strategies)"*. (Taylor & Loopstra 2016, 3).

This definition clearly suggests that food insecurity (at least in part) is a consequence of the kind of poverty that may lead to extreme ways of coping with tragic circumstances. Sadly, in relation to food security in the UK the Taylor and Loopstra report for The Food Foundation think tank also note that estimates suggest:

> *"...3.7 million people in the UK were living in moderately food insecure homes and 4.7 million people were living in severely food insecure homes in 2014, totalling 8.4 million"* (Taylor & Loopstra 2016, 4).

They also promote the requirement that the UK government should conduct more research in this area for longer term policy development to combat the worrying levels of the potential food insecurity issues which we face.

## UK Government and The Trussell Trust

Research commissioned by The Department for Environment, Food and Rural Affairs, and completed by Warwick University (2014), acknowledges the growth of the network of Trussell Trust Foodbanks in the UK, but also notes a diverse range of other projects providing food aid in communities. However, it also specifically notes that not all households in need of emergency food aid will seek support from such a network due to a number of different reasons including feelings of shame and degradation. Instead of asking for immediate help alternative strategies are put in place, which culminate in managing with less until it is impossible to manage any longer without support.

Being in the extremely difficult position of having no choice than to accept help in the form of emergency food support is often distressing for those individuals concerned. It is an emotion that is not lost on those who volunteer in the food aid services and nor are they immune to experiencing their own distress while supporting those in need. The UK Government Department for Digital, Culture, Media & Sport produced the Community Life Survey, which states that almost two-thirds of adults in the UK engaged with some form of volunteering during 2016/17 (Department for Digital, Culture, Media & Sport 2017). This army of individuals will have different reasons for giving their time and many have specific reasons for choosing particular charities. Food poverty is one issue that raises great concerns and this is substantiated by the Trussell Trust who note that more than 40,000 people in the UK chose to volunteer at foodbanks during 2015/16 (Trussell Trust – Volunteer with us 2019). Also, in joint research, the Trussell Trust and the Independent Food Aid Network in the UK (IFAN) found that individual volunteers around the UK are freely giving the equivalent of thirty million pounds (over four million hours) each year in unpaid support for local foodbanks (IFAN 2016). Food, as a basic survival requirement, is understood implicitly and thoughts of not having enough food for ourselves and our families conjures up primaeval anxieties about hunger, illness and mortality. As Winne (2008, xviii) makes note:

*"Food is the basic human necessity in which we invest the most energy to produce, and it unites the human race in a universal spirit of awareness, sharing, and charity".*

Concerns about food poverty have caused the number of foodbanks across the county to rise, and there has been a notable increase in the use of foodbanks in the North of England from 2011 to 2019 (Trussell Trust-Latest Statistics 2019). The largest network of foodbanks in the UK is coordinated by the Trussell Trust, however, independent charities, community groups and churches, also support local food aid projects. At this time, the UK government does not collect data on foodbank usage. The main source of data in this area is the Trussell Trust (House of Commons 2014). While it is remarkable that so much time is volunteered by those willing to pick up the responsibilities of community foodbank support, the message is clear that voluntary organisations are struggling, and that ultimate responsibility lies with the ruling government. IFAN's research notes that the Trussell Trust actively supports 1235 foodbanks in the UK and that there are more than 700 other independent foodbank locations (IFAN 2016). In addition to the unpaid hours volunteered each year, the Trussell Trust also note that ninety percent of the food they give out comes from public donations. It is made plain that the UK population is, by default, accepting the responsibility of providing foodbank resources. This has not gone unnoticed and the All-Party Parliamentary Inquiry into Hunger in the UK (2014, 5) acknowledges:

*"...marvellous work being carried out by volunteers which should be celebrated...tens of thousands of people have responded to real need by creating organisations such as food banks".*

Alongside the public are well-known large supermarkets that support food drives and supplement whatever the public donate with additional cash and goods. Also, people in positions of leadership and management in such corporations are now engaging with organisations such as the Global Food Banking Network and contributing to events such as the Food Bank Leadership Institute. This is a corporate approach which suggests that public policies should be developed further to support food producers and food retailers towards greater surplus food donation. As Winne (2008, xvii) remarks on the American perspective:

> "...our nation's approach to poverty has been to manage it, not to end it. And perhaps the best examples of good poverty management practices can be found in America's antihunger programs".

But the Global Food Banking Network do note the responsibilities of governments. In addition, the Trussell Trust and IFAN's joint research also makes clear that food poverty should not be a long-term voluntary or corporate obligation:

> "...voluntary organisations cannot replace the welfare state, the government must step up and take responsibility" (IFAN 2016).

The Social Metrics Commission (2018) reports that:

> "Currently there is no agreed UK government measure of poverty".

Also noted is that the EndHungerUK campaign report shows the UK Department for Work and Pensions Annual Food and Resources Survey will not be including a measure of food insecurity for some time, in fact:

*"The first datasets on household food insecurity will be available by March 2021".*

## Research and charities

Reviewing the literature uncovered research on some of the challenges facing charities overall. The UK Charities Commission (1995) suggest some of the difficulties that charitable organisations face are future planning, funding changes and governance changes, these are milestones which can cause crises. Also poor knowledge sharing and short-term solutions are noted as potential difficulties. The Charity Commission for Northern Ireland (2013) note that as a form of charity, foodbanks are an international reality and suggest that they will be a necessity for some time to come. Palmer (2012) recognises the need for professional management, and long-term strategic vision in regard to the sustainability of charity projects overall and in 2013, Noyes and Blond suggested:

*"...the Cabinet Office should introduce a new unit or taskforce..."*

This would help to explore the idea of working with churches for service delivery. However, contrary to this The Fabian Society's – Hungry for Change report (2015) determines that government should be planning to phase out foodbanks and work to bring household food insecurity to an end. This approach is supported by many and reported again by a number of academics referring to the charitable giving of food as a "sticking plaster" (The Guardian 2019).

There are a range of desperate situations which occur across the population that force people into using foodbanks. The AgeUK charity (2014) reported that

*"income poverty remains a critical issue for hundreds of thousands of pensioners...There are 1.6 million pensioners living in poverty in the UK...".*

AgeUK (2016) also note that the increase in the retirement age was placing further pressure on those approaching retirement who would not receive their pensions until much later than had been planned. Some cases had forced individuals to seek help from foodbanks. AgeUK help a number of older people who are not yet receiving a pension, and those experiencing problems with other state benefits who have also needed assistance from foodbanks. This highlights particular problems for older people who may not be strong enough to transport emergency food back to their own homes. Age UK (2014) reported a case where they were required to manage the visit of an elderly person to a foodbank as they would not otherwise have been able to attend. In addition, AgeUK (2015) reported a case where an older person had "great difficulty" carrying provisions home. At the other end of the age scale the children's charity, Barnardo's (2013), presented a report which suggested that:

*"Christmas dinner can often be a food parcel for many children".*

Barnardo's (2015) also reported on families with children who cannot manage without help from foodbanks due to low household income, with a Barnardo's service manager stating that one child explained how careful they are not to eat too much at home because he knows there isn't much.

In a briefing on Universal Children's Day (2015) Barnardo's continued to report that their family support services still see a reliance on foodbanks. In addition, the research of McEachern et al (2019) focuses on the movement of people in and out of emergency food need through different times of vulnerability. The valuable ongoing reporting of such need across the population certainly does not suggest improvement overall.

## UK, the North West and Manchester

The Trussell Trust is the largest foodbank network in the United Kingdom. The rise of UK foodbanks also coincided with the launch of the UK Government's "big society", which has been described by a Government aide as:

> "...empowering communities, redistributing power and fostering a culture of volunteerism...and acknowledged by Eric Pickles [British Conservative Party Politician] as-about saving money. If people are doing things for free then you don't have to pay public servants to do them for you." (Smith 2010)

Many faith groups are at the forefront of community engagement. The Church of England reports that it supports family, children and young people's activities by providing about 2,700 Church Staff and more than 80,000 volunteers (Church of England 2019). But, Loopstra et al (2015, 1) also note that charities may have "competing interest" which link to the expansion of their operations, pointing to concerns over fund raising in such cases. However, Devine (2003) notes that faith communities in the North West of England provide wide-ranging support through thousands of community projects which are supported by a huge force of more than 45,000 volunteers.

When stories of real need hit the headlines, such as that of foodbank use, the true requirements of actual survival are made plain. Inevitably this important social issue has become part of political rhetoric and the numbers of individuals and families using foodbanks has been reported in a number of contexts. Behind the reporting and the rhetoric, whether in or out of the news, foodbanks continue to provide essential services. However, it is the people working in foodbanks and giving continuous support for their communities who are the very fundament of this support network. They have the experience and understanding to express much more about foodbanks than that which creates a catchy headline. This community of service providers manage complex situations brought to them by individuals who are trying to overcome a range of life problems in order to survive from day to day. As noted by the charitable organisation Shelter (2016):

*"One in three working families are only one paycheque away from losing their home".*

A wide range of information in regard to foodbanks and other emergency provision is disseminated through news, books, research reports and from non-profit organisations. But also, in modern day dissemination practice, part of the backstory which aids our overall understanding of this topic is the information included in some areas of social media reporting, such as blogs and vlogs. Due to levels of poverty that may have been experienced for short or long periods of time by well-known personalities, some promote coping strategies within their expertise, such as cooking on a strict budget. Certainly, no-one can be said to be completely immune to potential financial catastrophe, but those that have little to begin with are in the most dangerous of positions.

Cooper and Dumpleton (2013) utilise a study by the Greater Manchester Poverty Commission which includes eight foodbank organisations in Manchester not linked to the Trussell Trust. These other organisations were:

*"...between them providing an average of 730 food parcels per month – equating to more than 8,700 per annum"*

This suggests that:

*"The evidence from Greater Manchester would indicate that the numbers of people reliant on food parcels is substantially higher than the figures supplied by the Trussell Trust, which are based solely on statistics gathered via their own food bank network"* (Cooper & Dumpleton, 2013, 5).

They also make note that there is no single central database for the number of foodbanks attributed to the Manchester area. In addition, the Indices of Deprivation Report (2015), Analysis for Manchester (2015/v1.1), presents Manchester as fifth in the ranking for the most deprived local authorities in England. Manchester is also ranked as fifth in the extent or spread of deprivation across the Indices of Deprivation measures, and seventh in the most deprived income domain.

Cooper and Dumpleton (2013, 3) called the growth in foodbank use in the UK "a national disgrace", and quote figures from the Trussell Trust to show the tripling in growth in foodbank use between 2012 and 2013 and at the time of their report, the Trussell Trust had approved 150 new foodbanks in the previous year. The data does not include that of similar independent organisations and, therefore, the partial picture in the Trussell Trust data could indicate a far larger problem which may one day overwhelm the capacity of voluntary organisations. Links between charities and social services are highlighted by the interest in such matters reported by some of our newspapers. Mason and Butler (The Guardian 2015) suggest that moves by Government to create closer relationships between job centres and foodbanks might instead generate greater mistrust between the job centres and the charities. Some, it is argued, would see a closer relationship as a loss of independence and there could be fears that funding might be impacted. Some foodbanks already refuse direct referrals from DWP job centres.

In the Trussell Trust regional breakdown for the financial year 2011/12, the total of people requiring assistance from foodbanks in the North West was 7,453. For the financial year 2012/13, the total leapt to 41,013. In 2013/14, the number grew to 138,644 and in 2014/15 this figure grew again to 157,248. The increase continued in 2015/16 to 160,048, and in 2016/17 to 174,489. For 2017/18 this number increased again to 197,182. The 2018/19 figure increased further to 222,722. The total is by far the highest of all regions in the UK (Trussell Trust Latest Statistics 2012-2019). The continuous and dramatic increases in the need for emergency food provision is a sad reflection on our times and highlight the need for the continued support of the foodbank workforce.

## Individual volunteers

While potential strategies to end food poverty may be negotiated by committees in high-level discussions, people at the grassroots community level continue the daily service to others of foodbank provision. This is reliant upon the continuous support of volunteer staff and individuals who are prepared to take on management responsibilities within volunteering, some of whom are volunteers themselves and others that may be paid. However, the research of Nesbit et al (2016) particularly notes that few organisations have individuals who are paid solely to take on the responsibility of managing volunteer staff. Whether or not there is paid or unpaid management taking overall responsibility, at the operations level, Finkelstein et al (2005) note that the effective day to day functioning of many organisations is dependent upon volunteers. The general concept of volunteering has a number of descriptors, which include simply offering to take part in a task or project, but more distinctly described by Scheier (1996) as:

*"Volunteering is doing more than you have to, because you want to, in a cause you consider good".*

Another descriptor by Volunteering Australia (2019) suggests that:

*"Volunteering is time willingly given for the common good and without financial gain".*

In addition, the National Council for Voluntary Organisations UK (2019) state that:

*"...volunteering...[is] any activity that involves spending time, unpaid, doing something that aims to benefit the environment or someone (individuals or groups) other than, or in addition to, close relatives".*

Many other descriptions of volunteering exist for some very specific groups such as older volunteers (Moore-McBride et al, 2012; Davis Smith & Gray 2005) and volunteering in widowhood (Shen & Perry 2016), while the more general term 'voluntary' is described in research by Salamon & Anheier (1992). But whatever the accepted definition of volunteering within particular contexts may be, there is also always the personal perspective of each volunteer, as Agostinho and Paco (2012, 251) note:

*"...different individuals can participate in the same type of volunteer work for very different reasons".*

As such, only personal stories can provide a detailed illustration of each individual's ongoing commitment to keeping the doors open for essential foodbank services. Although it is essential to recognise that volunteers do not necessarily suggest that foodbanks and other food aid services are a reasonable answer to the crisis of food insecurity. As reported in the All-Party Parliamentary Report (2014), volunteers advise on the importance of reducing demand for such services and recognising that many who are forced to accept the help of foodbanks are working families trying to manage on the minimum wage and benefit claimants who have to wait much too long for their claims to be processed. Such concerns are underlined by more than one foodbank in the All-Party Parliamentary Report indicating that high numbers of service users were in low paid work. The Joseph Rowntree Foundation (2019) also report that many families are:

*"locked in working poverty...across the UK...despite record levels of employment".*

Clearly, volunteers in food aid provision are supporting people and families across a varied social landscape. Indeed, the term foodbank has entered our common parlance and few require an explanation of its meaning. Sadly, many children are more than aware of what it means to them as:

*"Between 1 April 2018 and 31 March 2019, the Trussell Trust's food bank network distributed 1.6 million three-day emergency food supplies to people in crisis, a 19% increase on the previous year. More than half a million of these went to children".* (Trussell Trust End of Year Stats 2019)

Many foodbank volunteers are determined to do even more than provide food, while emergency food provision is the primary function of the service over time it has become obvious that many people, who are forced to use foodbanks, also require help with other practical matters and volunteers want to provide more support. Much of the spirit of this is recognised in the Trussell Trust initiative "More than Food". As they note (2019):

*"We support and encourage our food banks to provide compassionate, practical support to people in crisis to help better address the underlying causes of poverty".*

This suggests a much wider support network of help that may be accessed via volunteer support at foodbanks and elsewhere. These can be aspects of family life that would not usually be expected to have support, such as holiday clubs to help families through school holiday periods and courses to provide practical guidance on individual and family budgeting.

While some individuals choose to take on volunteering activities to improve their own skills and potentially their CV, just as many volunteers already have a number of professional workplace skills that they can bring into their volunteering practice. It is no bad thing that some people come to volunteering as a way of progressing themselves. Volunteering is not a one-way street and volunteers may also learn from service users, just as teachers may learn from students. We are none of us without knowledge to impart. Those that possess skills may wish to develop or gain other valuable skills in order to further their own progress and/or provide greater support to those in need. Whichever way this is perceived, there is an opportunity to develop individuals for society overall and volunteer organisations in particular.

## Discussion of the literature on foodbanks and volunteers

There are certain repeating themes across the literature written about foodbanks and reported upon here. Certainly, the Trussell Trust can be seen as a mainstay of emergency food support which operates country-wide and maintains a valuable support system for their large network of foodbanks. They also run an annual conference, produce yearly statistical reports and engage with innovative ideas to support foodbanks with more ways to contribute towards the social support of local communities. However, voluntary schemes are recognised as bodies which are plugging gaps left by the lack of social funding in some instances and, moreover, considered to be dealing with problems that have been caused by UK government benefit changes and limited support for families and individuals whether employed or unemployed. There are direct and indirect links from a foundation of austerity, which relate to all types of voluntary food provision, albeit foodbanks, soup kitchens or street food distribution. The steep increase in the use of foodbanks has sparked multiple conversations from many perspectives and the cause of such a rise in usage is highly debatable. The harsh impact of austerity measures has brought a much wider circle of service users to the foodbank service, many more than would have ever expected to be knocking on its door. Loopstra et al (2015, 2) comment that:

> "...more food banks are opening in areas experiencing greater cuts in spending on local services and central welfare benefits and higher unemployment rates. The rise in food bank use is also concentrated in communities where more people are experiencing benefit sanctions."

UK Government is now depending upon an unfunded and voluntary system to support those who have fallen outside the so-called safety net of our social service systems. Government have the important duty of rebalancing the way in which support can be arranged without overloading the voluntary sector further. In addition, social science research and charities recognise and report that food insecurity is a major issue which potentially impacts on us all and as such is a critical factor.

More themes than these come in and out of focus depending upon the perspective of each research project and every report. Sadly, one point of surety is that a greater range of factors will arise as the story of emergency food provision continues to evolve and becomes a normal part of daily life for some and no longer an unusual idea with our society. The United Kingdom is an apparent newcomer to the concept of foodbanks when compared with the United States of America, but during a relatively short space of time they have begun to plug a gap that seems only to widen. Questions about cause, consideration of effective systems, agreement and disagreement of right and wrong, and the resultant big decisions remain in the domain of Government. Meanwhile the volunteers continue to serve the people in need. They put into practice an alternative support network which is feeding the hungry, comforting the desperate, and giving more, much more than just food.

# CHAPTER 4

# PLACE AND THE NARRATIVE APPROACH–
# STORYTELLING

## The Investigation

Buchanan (2018, 277) specifically notes:

> *"Methodology affects what you see, how you see it, and what you do not see"*.

Therefore, context and methods should be transparent. The essence, the core, the spirit of this enquiry is based on the deep and heartfelt descriptions of the experiences of those who work in foodbanks in service of the people who need emergency food support. The context is within communities which recognise that some members of their community are in crisis. Need and abject poverty, as short and long-term problems, are ubiquitous in human history and true still in modern-day society. A running theme is the commitment of some to provide succour for those in need. That they do this is not in question, but why they do so, how it is enacted, who they are and who it is in turn that support their commitment to emergency support, is worthy of investigation. Knowledge of "why", provides intelligence for opportunities to engage with groups of potential future supporters. Understanding of "how" suggests possible improvements for both volunteer staff and service users. Consideration of "who", proposes types of management support that promote knowledge, experience and guidance for such valuable deeds. An investigation into the personal stories of the foodbank volunteers allows the why, how and who to naturally surface from the context and the rich descriptions of their varied experiences.

## Method and approach

Much consideration was given to method and approach before any contact was made with service providers, but the underlying essential was the unashamed intention to record the true and personal narrative of those who choose to serve by supporting their local community foodbanks. These are the people who meet and greet, authenticate referrals, converse with service-users to better understand their food needs and other issues with which they may require support, prepare food parcels, make tea, coffee and sandwiches, collect donations of food, stock the warehouse, shop for low stock items, and a number of other important day to day activities which ensure the survival of the foodbank services. Therefore, an interpretive interview approach was designated to collect, collate and present qualitative data from the narratives of foodbank service providers.

## Qualitative interviewing

As Bryman (2007, 465) notes:

*"The interview is probably the most widely employed method in qualitative research... it is the flexibility of the interview that makes it so attractive".*

Interviews as a research method have the potential to open a window into the life experience of individuals, but there are a number of differing techniques. In addition are legitimate concerns that an appropriate time and space should be sought for an interviewee to respond to questions and share information in a way that is most acceptable to them. Environments with people from different backgrounds and cultures can present communication issues, including how power is perceived in the interview relationship (Mullings 1999). Such factors may impact upon the type of information which respondents choose to share. There may also be potential embarrassment around some issues (Stommel & Willis 2004). Self-reflection is also a skill that supports the interview process and has relevance for the engagement of both the interviewer and interviewee, however, such a process is more natural to some than to others (Bassott 2016).

Structured interviews follow a prescribed pattern of questioning and are intended to collect definite answers to specified questions. This process gives little control to the interviewee and limited opportunities to stray from the path of questioning, which is dictated and managed by the interviewer. This is a useful formal format based on survey techniques that allows the collection of information from respondents who have all engaged with the same environment, interaction and set of questions. It supports the collection of specific answers for analysis and comparison and is, therefore, popular in quantitative approaches to research.

A greater degree of flexibility is provided through the semi-structured interview format which usually has, at its foundation, a list of questions.

These are delivered in a fairly informal way utilising a more general wording which gives scope for wider consideration. It also allows opportunities for the interviewer to consider the content of each answer and potentially include ad hoc questioning related to the interviewee's remarks. Semi-structured interviews are particularly useful when there are well-defined questions which evoke a response, but also engage the respondents in elaboration of the immediate first response.

Alternatively, if the purpose is to engage the interviewee in discussion, unstructured interviews support a loosely guided plan through points of interest. It is an informal process akin to a conversational approach. The order of addressing the points of interest may change for each interview to allow the delivery to appear natural within the scope of a discussion. The respondents may develop a particular storyline that allows the interviewer to discover much more detailed information than respondents have attributed in previous interviews. The delivery style is dependent upon the interviewer and interviewee combined. They are far less constrained when participating in this type of interview process.

Even greater freedom for both the interviewer and interviewee is embodied in the approaches that are based in the ethnographic tradition. Bound into research about human culture is also the enthusiasm to put information on record for posterity. But not just for that, also for the development of understanding of ourselves and the way in which we inhabit our world. Documented accounts of cultural groups are a strong theme in the history of the ethnographic approach and this work often comes from researchers immersing themselves within an environment.

These social study experiments support deeper investigation and understanding of a time and place and provide useful opportunities for organisational research. However, a researcher may not have the opportunity to engage with this style of participant observation for an extended length of time, in one group or organisation, in order to record a person's life history or even part of it. If this is the case biographic narrative, which also has its roots in ethnography, provides the opportunity to engage with those individuals that are willing to impart their story to an enthusiastic listener. The biographic narrative interviewer offers an interview environment which extends much of the control to the interviewee. Wengraf (2007) offers a detailed explanation of practice and interpretation of Biographic Narrative Interpretive Method (BNIM) for use as a complete approach. However, the method has even wider appeal as parts of the technique can support other narrative approaches towards general storytelling by those who have expert knowledge and experience of a specific place and/or context. This study embraces elements of BNIM to consider narratives of a volunteer workforce.

## BNIM in the context of this study

Long before the issuing of invitations to potential interviewees, researchers must consider their approach in the context of their research. Such contexts may conjure memories of experiences that are difficult or upsetting to narrate. As such, consideration of a sympathetic approach is necessary. A relaxed environment is preferable and the researcher should seek to be supportive, but not lead the narration. Here the data collection process was guided by elements of the Biographic Narrative Interpretive

Method, which offers a supportive framework but leaves space for the individual narrative of each person to be presented. BNIM was chosen as an approach due to this method's prior success in revealing the narratives from interviewees' lives (Wengraf 2001, 2004). The traditional approach of BNIM is the construction of a primary question or statement, known as the Single Question aimed at Inducing Narrative (SQUIN), this was developed for use in the interviews for this study. In this instance the question was framed as follows:

*"Can you please tell me your own story of your experience of working in a foodbank?"*

Questions of this type avoid limiting responses to a few defined points and encourage the telling of a full and personal story. The interviewer refrains from speaking, which creates the space for the participant's voice to be privileged (Smith 2012). The interviewee chooses what they wish to share and how their individual story is portrayed. The interviewee is given space to continue until the story seems to approach a natural end. They are then prompted by the researcher who reintroduces specific events or incidents from the narrative and asks the interviewee to elaborate further, these prompts are known as Particular Incident Narratives (PINs). PINs are answered by further reflection on what has already been said. This often encourages more detailed commentary.

A specific objective of this study was to uncover the untold stories of volunteers providing emergency food services. To this end rich descriptions, through the application of the Biographic Narrative Interpretive Method, were recorded and evaluated. The BNIM interview method allowed interviewees to present their own experiences as free as possible from any researcher bias and recorded the rich descriptions of their individual experiences.

Smith (2012, 3) particularly notes BNIM as a:

*"...powerful methodology for capturing lived situations and experiences through narrative interviewing"*

In this instance, the open-ended narrative approach led into a final short section where respondents were asked to consider a few simple practice and theory-driven questions. Such questions in the field are appropriate where respondents have a: *"...complex stock of knowledge"* (Flick 2006, 155).

On completion of the interview process each narrative was transcribed and the constant comparison technique, recommended for the analysis of statements by Bogdan & Biklen (1982), was utilised to investigate each narrative. Provisional categories were allocated based on the first transcript and, where possible, remarks of the next and all subsequent respondents were allocated to the original categories. New categories were created as required, which led to a set of categories that allowed the specific organisation of the main points.

As previously noted, interviews were conducted with service providers from six foodbanks in the North West of England. Respondents totalled sixteen in number. Some had been working at the foodbanks for a few months, but the majority had been involved with foodbanks and other charitable services for many years. The majority of respondents had professional backgrounds in social work, law, community outreach and nursing. Given the range of experience in their present voluntary posts, and in most cases extensive prior experience, there were no grounds for supposing that the respondents were not competent to voice meaningful narratives.

The North West of England has seen a dramatic increase and sustained year on year growth in the use of foodbank services. It is also ranked as an area of significant deprivation and while these are important factors, of equal significance are the lengths to which volunteers and community support organisations go to in order to help and support those who are suffering most as a result of overall deprivation.

The Biographic Narrative Interpretive Method, as interview method, supported the collection of the interview information. BNIM in conjunction with the constant comparison technique of analysis provided five specific categories for investigation; reasons for volunteering; organising the service; organisational difficulties/limitations; practical and emotional support; and the future of foodbanks.

# Resulting details from the investigation of the narratives and questionnaires

This investigation proffered two types of opportunity when reporting on the resulting information. The usual approach is to present sections specific to each of the categories which emerged and detail the relevant points with some use of anonymous quotations from respondents. This opportunity is realised in chapter 5 (The narratives). However, the abundance of detailed qualitative information about this important social context and the particular situational knowledge provided deserves greater attention. This is not only due to the richness of the narratives, but also to the unexpected occurrence of recording the story of one service which was situated outside the normal description of a foodbank service. As such, following the usual analysis of emerged categories in chapter 5 (The narratives), and in order to give due recognition to an entrepreneurial approach and the potential for innovation in foodbank services, further specific reporting is provided in chapter 6 (The outlier).

In addition to the analysis by categories and further reporting, there is also some additional information from the basic questionnaires that were completed by the respondents.

## Analysis of questionnaires

When the individual narratives came to a natural end, each respondent was asked to comment on a short list of practice and theory-driven questions related to the field. These questions simply enquired about the following factors: Age, Educational Background, Training received and further training wanted. All sixteen respondents chose to complete the short questionnaire.

### Age

In the age range 20-29, there were five responses.

In the age range 40-49, there was one response.

In the age range 50-59, there were two responses.

In the age range 60-69, there were four responses.

In the age range 70-79, there were four responses.

## Educational background

Eleven out of sixteen respondents had prior management qualifications and/or management training. This ranged from work experience in the NHS, charities, the law, city councils, social work, the probation service, teaching, nursing, counselling, and general management.

Whether they had received training (via the foodbank)

Eight out of sixteen respondents had received some training and stated that it was useful to have done so. From the eight that did not receive any training, five would have liked the opportunity to engage in training.

If they would value the opportunity to engage with further training, and what kind of training they would consider most useful.

Nine respondents specifically highlighted the type of training they thought would be most helpful. These included: in-house data/computer training, business planning, marketing, and fundraising. The most repeated themes were: information about other support agencies, welfare benefits and accommodation, social care and immigration.

## Conclusion

The way in which this study was operationalised supports a transparent approach to research in social contexts. The methods and engagement with the respondents in this case have been clearly detailed. The many and varied reasons for engaging in such community support (suggested throughout the narratives) complement other research which provides intelligence in this area. Overall descriptions provided by respondents on the day to day support, furnished by volunteers, give information to guide possible improvement of the services. Importantly, with a view to supporting the future development of the service, both the narratives and the questionnaire responses give some indication of an interest in training and management. This collection and investigation of the personal stories of foodbank volunteers was enabled by the sensitive methods recommended in the use of the narrative approach in social science research.

# CHAPTER 5

# THE NARRATIVES

As noted in the previous chapter, five specific categories emerged via the narrative interview method employed in this investigation: reasons for volunteering, practical and emotional support, organising the service, organisational difficulties/limitations, and the future of foodbanks.

## Analysis through five emerged categories

### Category: reasons for volunteering

The narratives of the foodbank volunteer workers note that they have their own reasons for giving their personal time. Some are time-rich due to retirement or only part-time work commitments, but there are also a number of busy individuals with full-time jobs and family obligations who still find it possible to commit a regular number of hours to charitable and community causes. The individual narratives, which provide the foundation for this book, tell stories of some commonality. Many of the volunteers have professional backgrounds in social work, nursing, law and education. They tend to volunteer within their own communities because they have recognised a need that is not being met by other services. However, there are also some decidedly uncommon reasons for volunteering, such as acknowledging a personal lack of social and communication skills and wishing to improve these through service to others or feeling that a life of advantage requires some form of recompense to a less privileged group, and also wanting to give something back to a service due to feelings of enormous gratitude after being supported by that service. A wide range of individuals exist within the context of volunteer groups and despite the misgivings that many have about the limitations of the services offered, they provide continued support for these community enterprises ad infinitum. Reasons for initially volunteering are often linked with other relationships, such as belonging to a church or faith group that decides to branch out into a form of general community service. Engagement through church groups and experience of previously volunteering are positive factors for many in this unpaid workforce. Perspectives of working alongside likeminded individuals, who want to practice their faith by helping those in need, is a strong theme for those associated through faith groups. However, some volunteers are not connected to their volunteer ethos through church links and clearly note that it is important to them to say that they are not committed for any religious reasons. Some volunteers with no connection to churches or faith groups express the difficulties they have encountered when trying to find a secular emergency food provider with which to volunteer. None had been able to locate what they considered to be a secular foodbank.

## Category: organising the service

Volunteer groups are an unpaid workforce that often plug modern-day gaps in our social services. As important as that human workforce is, it is equally important to have a store of goods which are donated for general distribution. While many large and small organisations take a philanthropic approach to donating goods and funds, this unstable supply chain can be a cause for concern. Volunteers name supermarkets as some of the most generous donators.

These large donations are facilitated by the Trussell Trust foodbanks, which have a national partnership, enabling food drives that are organised by the large supermarket chains. They allow an allocation of days each year for dedicated food collections at stores around the country. In addition, many supermarkets also have permanent foodbank collection points and give oversupplied items to foodbanks. The gratitude engendered by such opportunities is clearly expressed by volunteers experiencing the food drive:

> *"You would not believe how generous people are...one lady brought a trolley full". "To be at [the supermarket] this morning was life-enhancing. The baskets...really build up and whatever is given, [the supermarket] give 30% more. So, it's the great British public. The supermarkets give and...some people say its vested interest, but I say its benevolence...the last big collection of food was four and a half tons".*

Volunteers also sometimes experience ad hoc deliveries from food manufacturers in their region and these can be substantial donations, as explained here:

> *"[One] sent pallets of cereal and just before Christmas [another] sent boxes of chocolates for the volunteers. But there were loads, so we gave them out. At Easter they sent very posh Easter Eggs. People were very appreciative".*

Items that are seen as additional or extra to the normal provisions are considered important as suggested here:

*"It's so nice when you have got some sort of extra things that are not the basics, extra things for the kids-crisps, chocolate biscuits, drinking chocolate, they really appreciate it".*

The volunteer groups that are connected to a specific church also note their churches and parishioners as very generous and crucial to many foodbanks:

*"Most of the food comes from church",*

*"churches give fairly hefty donations of food each month",*

*"Once a month we have a food collection at church because sometimes the cupboard can almost be bare".*

The support provided by some churches is also financial:

*"our manager knows that he can access some money for people who are in dire straits, usually for money owed on utilities".*

Other benevolent organisations include local schools, hospitals and banks. They are noted as kind contributors to foodbanks. Local small businesses also provide goods and financial support. However, the volunteers regularly and readily comment on the "Great British public" and how their generosity appears to know no bounds.

*"Individuals don't just donate via supermarket food drives, 'People give financially too…", "People are very kind".*

Nonetheless, that which may not be widely known or even considered is the volume of donations made by the volunteers themselves. Volunteers as a category of donators should not be forgotten. Many volunteers recognise which products are regularly depleted and seek to redress the balance to prevent foodbank users from going without.

> *"Volunteers also bring things in if they know we are running low".*
> *"Toothpaste isn't a basic, but if I see cheap toothpaste I grab it... because it makes a person feel better".*

Volunteer workers at foodbanks understand that emergency food provision is an issue that impacts on the many rather than the few and is succinctly noted here by a volunteer:

> *"The whole community understands that food poverty is a tragedy and an issue that... is on the national conscience and ...is too big to be ignored...".*

While an unpaid workforce can enable the continuation of a service and partially support it through the supply of a basic provision of goods, there is no doubt that there are obvious limitations which must be recognised.

## Category: organisational difficulties/limitations

Foodbank volunteers accept that there are limitations built into the service:

> *"I don't like the bureaucracies of systems around vulnerable people and people in poverty. It just gets more and more degrading".*

But an understanding of some rules was also apparent:

*"The Trussell Trust training seemed very prescriptive, but Trussell Trust is tried and tested, ...if it's a charity you have to be more accountable than even your own business. But...we have lots of volunteers from professional backgrounds and we know how to work as a group. The food values are worked out for amounts required, what is sufficient, these are all worked out by the Trussell Trust dieticians. So the food value of what is required is for one person, and its three meals per day for three days, that's what they get. But, if it is one person getting food for a family of four, you can see if there are any extras to add in. We stick to the rules, but the system is elastic enough...If they need a hot meal we send them to Cornerstones[1]".*

While there are some reservations about rules, there is also clear recognition that procedures are required to safeguard the sustainability of foodbanks:

*"At the start it wasn't very good, it was hanging on by a thread and I didn't think it would stay open. But the Trussell Trust came along and explained what we needed to do to improve, everything changed".*

Although there are clear constraints that are understood, volunteers have a front row view of the practical implications of emergency food provision. They hear heart-rending explanations about the way in which some individuals in our society are struggling to survive from day to day. In consideration of how things might change, some volunteers suggest extending what is on offer:

---

[1] A Roman Catholic centre 'providing services to vulnerable and disadvantaged adults...Cornerstones welcomes people from all backgrounds' http://cornerstonecds.org.uk/about-us/

*"It would be good to be able to have fresh food to give out, bread and vegetables. We aren't allowed to accept fresh food or give it out, it's a rule".*

However, in contrast, the long-term sustainability of foodbanks is also in the forefront of the minds of volunteers:

*"We have a bunch of volunteers and donated food. Basically, once you have enough people who know what they are doing it just seems to work. But, Government is not willing to give money directly to those in need, so they aren't going to give it to foodbanks. People are referred to other charities too. But in the long run I'm not sure how sustainable it is... I am worried that in the future foodbanks will close. Resources are stretched, if the number of people who need foodbanks increases and the available volunteers decrease it won't be sustainable".*

It can be seen that the commitment of these volunteers stretches to far more than a few hours each week supporting the practice of emergency food provision. They are fully engaged and feel a sense of ownership. They have deep concerns about the severe predicaments experienced by those who need the service, overwhelming gratitude for those who supply goods and financial support and grave concerns about the future of this vital service.

Some extreme situations are noted regarding the sustainability of provisions:

*"We have never run out of pasta or beans which is good because they are two staples, but we regularly run low on tinned fish, tinned meat, tinned fruit, rice pudding, milk, sugar and fruit juice, all of which are important for a balanced diet. We have been surviving by topping up the shopping with a*

*grant we got from the local council".*

Commentary of volunteers also reveals potentially stressful situations:

*"...one Christmas we were literally giving people baked beans. I was shocked, but people were really grateful. We realised we had to sort things out, it just wasn't working, but it's sorted now. We have a lot of fund-raising activities-we do get food and money coming in and we have an emergency fund. It's working quite well".*

Also noted are the sometimes challenging physical requirements and concerns about the health of older volunteers:

*"Our resources are really stretched so senior volunteers have taken on a lot of responsibilities and made really good decisions".*

*"...we need more able-bodied young people for collections and the warehouse. The people in our store say they are ok, but most have back issues, we could do with help for lifting and handling".*

Also required are specific expertise:

*"We could do with someone who is interested in focusing on getting money, using publicity and negotiating access to more drop box areas. We need experience and expertise in strategic financial focus, fund-raising and publicity".*

## Category: practical and emotional support

When speaking about individual contact, a variety of situations arose:

*"Every week people come in here and they are desperate, embarrassed and ashamed. We sort out food, signpost them to other organisations. They are*

*so grateful and thankful and say 'I don't know what we'd have done without you, my kids are going to be so pleased' that's the kind of thing you remember"*.

It is noted that many foodbanks are limited to offering three food parcels as emergency provision, and that is something that volunteers *"just have to accept"* as it is *"food for a time of crisis"*.

There is general satisfaction about the level of training received, particularly at Trussell Trust supported foodbanks and volunteers appreciate the opportunity to *"try everything"* such as:

*"... the front desk, checking each voucher that comes in, the stockroom...making up bags of food to match preferred goods (pasta or rice, tea or coffee, whether they are vegetarian or not)"*.

However, there is also some frustration around food regulation:

*"If we have things that are out of date we are not allowed to give them because of food hygiene, but people can take it at their own risk and they really appreciate it. There are some stupid hygiene laws"*.

Foodbank managers were often spoken of as supportive and highly knowledgeable:

*"Our manager tries to sort out housing problems, benefits, even legal things"*.

A great deal of praise and respect was stated, especially the care they show for volunteers, one expressing the importance of feedback:

*"On a day-to-day basis, our manager is very good at managing situations and keeping up morale and keeping in touch with what is happening with clients. He updates us on their stories when he has spoken to the referrer so that we get the bigger picture of what is really going on, which is really good because then we know it's not just about giving food...".*

The admiration felt for the managers was specifically expressed and in the words of two volunteers:

*"...there should be more help for people involved in managing and running foodbanks",*

*"...the manager here is great at managing volunteers and morale, and how everything works. I think it's fantastic".*

In addition, the managers may also have to deal with the harsh realities of what might be termed potential abuse of the system:

*"...our manager is a wealth of information, I don't know how we'd function without him, he is amazing. There is a negative side to meeting the clients when there is perhaps one who is obviously abusing the system. I find that difficult to handle, but our manager deals with such situations very well".*

Managers are particularly noted for their people-management skills:

*"Our manager asks us before we open the foodbank what we want to do that day...we are never left not knowing what to do".*

Some volunteers noted that more training, especially regarding emotional issues, would be useful, but also noted that:

*"...many of the volunteers already have an awful lot of training and experience".*

However, one volunteer had concerns about:

*"...discussing quite disturbing situations...and...not [being] comfortable with the religious element".*

Less experienced volunteers also spoke about their first foray into foodbank support as initially *"terrifying...and [being] embarrassed"* when talking to strangers in difficult circumstances.

*"It can be upsetting when clients come in, there are a lot of sad stories and people are ashamed".*

It was suggested that further specific training in relation to what is available locally might be useful, but all felt able to hand over to their manager for more assistance, as noted here:

*"First you find yourself wishing you had more knowledge, but then start wishing that the system just worked better".*

The overriding theme communicated by the volunteers was:

*"Our training instils in us that we aren't here to judge anyone. We do all we can to help and try never to let anyone go empty-handed."*

## Category: the future of foodbanks

While volunteers had many concerns about the future and how foodbanks could continue, their fears of government intrusion were even stronger:

*"It's been said that government-run foodbanks might come in. This is scary*

*because no-one knows how they will be controlled".*

Others suggested that: *"Government would just make it into another system...[and] people fall through the holes..."* and *"there is safety in autonomy".* Also, *"...people will not feel comfortable going there..."*, so the clear view was that foodbanks should be *"seen as independent with no particular axe to grind".*

An important and very personal insight was provided by one previous service user who is now a foodbank volunteer: *"I don't think things should change. It's the volunteers that are beautiful and kindly and make it a peaceful place. Then it will always be a place where there is help and a place where there are solutions when you are in big difficulties".*

Many volunteers wished that

> *"...foodbanks could be more welcoming, friendly, café-like...drop-in spaces with a foodbank attached".*

Also, a system that allows people to:

> *"...choose their own food' and: 'combine with other support services to provide more than food".*

Some volunteers had attended a conference held by the Trussell Trust and were pleased to hear about possible initiatives, such as:

> *"providing suits for people to go to job interviews",* and *"...setting up furniture stores for furniture restoration...".*

Other ideas included:

*"[home] deliveries"*,

*"a food club with a big pan of soup on the go"*,

*"a wider service, benefits advice, work advice, referrals to agencies that can offer further support…"*,

*"there is clothing need and furniture"*,

*"…it would be nice if we could do meals, give a bit more than just tins to take home. There are ones in Manchester, Cornerstones, the Catholic one, they are very good the Roman Catholics. You can spend the day there, have all your meals for free, you can't sleep there, but you can have a shower. It would be nice to have more places like that…".*

Even though concerns were voiced about long term sustainability, there was overwhelming agreement that foodbanks would always be needed:

*"I think there will always be gaps and people at the bottom who even struggle to fill in a form. There's a lot going on with foodbanks, some are starting…to help people use food wisely…We don't have cooking lessons at school…which is silly because it is a life skill….I would imagine that more and more people will be coming through the door, so busier is what I think it will look like in the future"*, and *"…there will always be people who slip through the net, they will need emergency support; women fleeing from domestic violence, problems for people moving around and not able to access benefits…I'd like to see foodbanks in every local area so that everyone is in walking distance of a foodbank…if people are struggling to buy food then getting on a bus is going to be difficult"*. School holidays were also recognised as a time of additional difficulty for some families: *"Benefit cuts mean that in the holidays, when children are at home, parents have the pressure of covering the meals that would be free school meals"*.

Volunteers recognised the Trussell Trust model as empathetic to their community and relevant to voluntary practice:

*"...the Trussell Trust is a good model if we can keep it small enough to a community that helps people to be more productive. I suspect we will have foodbanks for the rest of my life. It's to do with financial situations- maximum mortgages, children, payday loans, ...there will always be times like this".*

Even further, comments highlight the wide-ranging nature of need which is presented across communities and while many volunteers see their support activities as a long-term commitment, there is sadness regarding the need for foodbanks and how they are sometimes perceived:

*"I don't see things changing, hopefully donations will increase, but that depends upon people realising that it is not about the feckless, these people have very genuine problems and it could happen to a member of your family".*

Also:

*"...surely, there should be a way of making sure that people do not run out of food... the UK is supposedly a developed country. People on benefits are always blamed and it would take a big cultural shift for that to change...I think foodbanks of the future should be like nice shops, so it's not a poverty thing, ... But really, people don't need foodbanks, they need well paid jobs so that they can earn. People don't want to come to foodbanks, but they have no choice".*

These narratives portray the requirement for a multi-faceted response to support foodbank users;

*"[it's] an eye-opening experience when you come face to face with individuals and the situations they are in. You just listen and try to screen for the problems that you can help with... there is a lot [of] help... but it's not connected-up. Everyone knows the statutory stuff because of Social Services but Housing Associations are providing so much more, such as money management and sometimes buying out loans. Community centres are also providing lunch clubs, activity clubs, youth clubs, wellbeing where you can get access to clothes and toys. Family Support Officers have kids referred to them and they investigate how they can support the family. Children are sometimes living between parents who might have other care responsibilities for older relatives. They may not be coping well financially and might need emergency food while things are sorted out. Sometimes teachers see that children in their class are hungry and then more of the story evolves of a family whose father is in prison and benefits were in his name, so the wife has nothing and can't feed the children. Other situations can be children with special needs or exclusions from school and women who do not get benefits in their own right... we have had situations where a partner has died, and women may be left with babies and no rights to benefits or housing. There are some very sad cases, some people come and sit in the foodbank just because they feel safe here".*

The narrative of the foodbank as a place of safety and friendship is also emphasised by the words of another volunteer:

*"We chat and sometimes find that they have other problems. When they have finished their drink and are ready to go they take their carrier bags. We have one person who just comes in for a cup of coffee. He has some mental health problems and just wants to chat. He has a couple of coffees and a chat and then he just drifts off when he is ready. We have helped him in the past, and his benefits are sorted out now, but he just comes in for a chat"*

The one-time foodbank user, who is now a volunteer, sensitively explains why the foodbank is not simply about food:

> *"It was like opening the doors to a big family when I came here. I remember how they helped me... The food was important because I needed it, but the biggest help is the people".*

The narratives given by the foodbank volunteers range from practical statements to heart-rending testaments of those who endeavour to provide assistance and friendship. The descriptions of service-users depict many who are in dire need and have nowhere else to turn. Environments created to cope with modern day food shortages evoke strong emotions. So too does the experience of working in such environments. Just as the foodbanks are not only about food, the volunteer workers are not just about volunteering. They bring their whole selves into this environment and carry the knowledge of the place and the people. For many, working with a group of like-minded people is important, but even more so is knowing that their manager will be there to do what they cannot, and that nobody will go away empty handed.

# CHAPTER 6

# THE OUTLIER

Having considered the existing norms of community foodbanks that have been portrayed thus far, we now turn to one which defies the usual description. Just one of the foodbanks included in this study was neither a Trussell Trust foodbank, nor connected to any church or faith group. This is unusual in itself, but of interest too is the story of the founder, who had a personal mission to give support, but not within the confines of that which was already available through other services. Reflections on his earlier home life related elements of family crisis and a deep understanding of helping others without any judgement in the way that good friends may offer assistance without requiring any evidence of dire need. This proactive and caring man explains that he has never suffered extreme poverty, but his father died when he was quite young which forced a move to a new home that required renovation. His mother was coping with bereavement and the needs of three young children. He recalls that there were cards and flowers from the neighbours, but his mother recalled how different it was in the past when she lived on a local council estate. She recalled times of difficulty, such as bereavement, when:

*"... neighbours would say 'sorry for your loss' but also do something practical, bring a casserole, do the washing, cook for the kids, give a bit of*

*money and tell you it's not a loan and not to worry about it"*.

He recalls his mother's reflections of living on a private estate, which was very different because people brought

*"lots of cards and flowers, but that was it"*.

This young man's early life experiences heightened his recognition of the extreme difficulties that many people face. His altruistic approach links to an interest in working within the charity sector in order to help others. He has worked with homeless people on outreach programmes and in other foodbanks. He recalls that many of the people he came into contact with who were living on the streets had mental health problems. He was enthusiastic about one volunteer in particular:

*"...one of the main volunteers is a therapist and talks to a lot of service users in depth and gets [returning] service users on the outreach programme. They come back every month and want to talk to him. Because of that I thought about the type of profession that would give me the opportunity to, I don't know how to put this-give a shit! My brother hears voices and his biggest fear was being sectioned. My mum has helped him to manage"*.

The experiences related here give some insight into this man's decision to support his local area through a non-traditional approach to emergency food support and much more. However, finding a way to do so was not as simple as we might think. He had the support of his partner who was also very closely connected to the community that they call home. She explained her own background and why she also felt that local support was vital:

*"I come from a close-knit family, my mum, sister, auntie, and their kids. Also, I'm a teaching assistant. As a woman, watching other women struggle is hard, you also see how some families segregate themselves from the ones that are poor, it's a diffusion of responsibility. But then at the foodbank you see that sometimes the people with the least give the most. I've had a fortunate life, I grew up in a small community, I have never seen this level of poor people before, but other people do rally round to support them. There wasn't one main reason why I came to work at the foodbank, but it was nice to be there with my partner, he's like a different person at the foodbank, it's lovely to see him there. I am a weak-willed person, but at the foodbank you know you are doing something good. You see the split of higher, middle and lower class all over again. The cost of living is rising and people's wages are not. We will need more foodbanks. I think by 2020 90% of the UK will have accessed a food bank at least once. It makes us sound like a third world country".*

While this young woman's affiliation to the foodbank is stated mainly in support of her partner, she provides insightful understanding of the way in which even short-term financial crisis can destroy family networks, but also the observable value of doing good for both those who give and receive.

## Finding a place to do good

In his steadfast but approachable manner, the young man says:

*"I'm an atheist, I have no selected faith. I wanted to be involved in charity work, preferably something to do with homelessness. So, I contacted Salvation Army and a few others. They are all faith-based and while I was talking to them on the phone it was explained that I could not be a volunteer because I don't have their faith. I said that I'm not anti-religion and wouldn't*

*penalise anyone that does believe. I just want to help".*

His views on some traditional forms of charitable assistance are keen and provide further understanding of his non-traditional approach:

*"Churches don't want to help, they want recognition for helping. When I spoke at church meetings [in an attempt to gain support for a non-traditional foodbank project] one of the arguments was that they were already doing things-renovating a park and other things. But why would you prioritise a park? They thought that they were doing enough because they worked full-time and do charity work! But, to a non-religious person, I just think that theirs is a calling so shouldn't it be 24/7? I work full-time and volunteer too. Why are church rooms empty at night and at weekends? If this is a test why aren't they doing better, more? Why are you wearing jewellery, why have you got a gold crucifix round your neck? Surely, you don't need a symbol of your faith if you are providing for another human being. I think as an ethos, a philosophy, a religion; Islamic, Judaism, Christianity, Buddhism, whatever, the philosophy is help someone and don't be a dick! And I don't think many people do that, they just want their own groups. Christians will look after Christians, or they will all go out to the homeless, provide them with food, but then pray! Well of course they will pray and say Jesus is my saviour if they want to eat! During Ramadan I went out with the Muslims to feed the homeless, no-one prayed or did anything like that. At the end of Ramadan everyone was invited to break the fast with them in Piccadilly Gardens. They were just giving out food, but there was a Christian preacher there all the time shouting. We have approached the preachers before and said 'you don't need to talk about it, just come and help us hand out the food, there might be Christian people here that would want to speak to you that you can give some comfort to'. But the answer is always that God doesn't want me to do that, he wants me to do this. One*

*preacher tried to convert me, which I don't mind, he comes on the outreach with the street workers and I think that's good. A friend of mine who is an evangelical Christian doesn't do any of that, he just involves himself in it directly. I think any person who wants to justify their actions in religion should be helping more. If they are performing outreach three times a week, why aren't they doing four? I know I sound awful but, I don't believe it's a test. I don't believe there is anything better than this... People get annoyed when I attend church meetings because I sound flippant when I say-'don't be a Christi-can't, be a Christi-can. Why do you need a church, a doctrine, you have your own moral compass?' It's not pressure, people say volunteering is demanding, but all you're doing is giving someone a bag of food. It's not hard, you haven't paid for the food. I just think they just want to be recognised for doing good... That's probably what annoys me the most about religion, they are in it for the big reward because there is some magic place. I've got a lot of contempt for people who don't want to help-that's my issue. I don't mean money, [you can] donate food, donate time. My biggest issue is the diffusion of responsibility. Why should I help, the government should do that, I pay my taxes, or we've got to speak to the church! But you can just make a decision, be your own supervisor, why can't you allow a donation point, how will you be penalised for that? I think if Jesus was here himself and you [think] he might tell us off? What, for helping the poor? I think he would say, 'what's wrong with you?' [But] I think people are too afraid of being punished or blamed for something, which makes them not able to help. It's just daft!"*

He continued his search for a place where he might help others away from the confines of traditional charitable support. Eventually he happened upon an organisation which had been founded, in the main, by Islamic members. However, faith was not a barrier, all faiths were welcome. He describes how engagement with the group began:

*"When I arrived I realised it was just Muslims and then me, but we didn't talk about faith, we focused on providing care packages to homeless people. We also did foodbank support which [supported] up to twenty organisations. Some places had specific client groups such as asylum seekers, refugees, women fleeing domestic violence. These were all supported. Subsequently, these places found different suppliers for the stock they needed and also funding. So we decided to open a foodbank, mainly because a lot of foodbanks only open on Mondays and Fridays and they have to operate solely on referrals, and there is a finite amount of food people are allowed to receive in a specific period. We thought there were people in work and outside the benefit system who might need one-off help of consistent support for a full month to get on their feet. So that's what we were trying to identify. I tried to [set up an associated foodbank] in my [community]. There are five local churches ranging from Catholic, Protestant to Jehovah's Witness, but none of them wanted to be involved. I then went to a community meeting, there were MPs and local business people present. I explained that we needed a [local] storage facility that we could use for free. I was offered a massive storage facility, but the next day I was told that due to my affiliation with a Muslim group we wouldn't be given the storage space. The local businessman spoke of wanting to help with the foodbank because he had been through hard times himself and been brought up in poverty, but still did not feel he could help. Eventually a local children's nursery gave us a storage room for free. So we moved the stock there. They were already aware of potential service users because they were in daily contact with the children, then [staff at the nursery] became people who would distribute [food parcels] too. So, it made sense".*

The initial independent foodbank project continued with the timely help of the storage facility provided by the children's nursery. It provided support for a wide range of ages from eighteen to over eighties. A number of referrals arrived from groups such as Age Concern and local schools. The message that the foodbank was open and would be pleased to take referrals was communicated to local churches. This reaching out created greater understanding of the project and every church agreed to be a dropping off/donation point where local businesses and the community could donate provisions, and they also received cash donations. This collaborative approach is recalled as a useful period for the alternative/non-traditional foodbank which sought to help a wider range of the community than was usually associated with foodbank use. Support did not require the premise of a social service referral:

*"Sometimes people would phone up and say 'can I self-refer' and they were so accustomed to quantifying how poor they are, they would say 'what questions do you need to ask', and then I'd say 'have you got bread and milk now, or do I need to get to you in the next half hour? Can you wait until tomorrow? How many kids have you got and how old are they, I'm only asking because there is no use me just giving you enough food for young children, if you have teenagers you will need more'. And people found it really refreshing that it was such a sensible approach and surprised that we gave fresh bread, a choice of red, green or blue milk, butter and eggs".*

*"The community was working together. I think there is a common misconception that people squander their benefits and end up at the foodbank. My experience is that working-class families have sudden financial impacts such as the car stops working, a family member becomes long-term sick or leaves the household, children are on school holidays*

*which means they miss breakfast club, [free school] dinners, etc. Depending upon the size of the family you could potentially have to find up to an extra thirty meals per week. So those are the aspects we decided to help cover. Most foodbanks provide non-perishable and dry items because they are easy to donate and store. So, that's what we did initially".*

Other differences to the traditional foodbank service included the delivery of food and personal hygiene products. In order to avoid embarrassment to the service users it was decided that there would be no use of logos or branding. Goods were delivered from an ordinary car in generic shopping bags as though a friend was dropping things off. The delivery option was also seen as imperative due to the lack of client funds:

*"...if someone hasn't got enough money to buy value beans, they definitely haven't got bus fare...we arranged a time ...and even had a give back process, so if there were things in the food parcel that they couldn't use they could return it and we would redistribute it. We also supported small requests like red, green or blue milk and people were thankful for that. At one point we were given hundreds of travel shower gel packs, so we started including them with the food packs and people wanted them".*

Other innovative ideas included detailed leaflets on debt advice and benefit claims, drop-in centres, and contact information for government welfare offices. All leaflets were printed on both sides, one with details for those who may need help and the other specifying how to make donations to the foodbank. This was a specific strategy to avoid stigmatizing service users. No-one could be identified either as a person who needed the service or someone that was simply wanting to donate to the service, the leaflet could be kept for either purpose (or both).

## Clients

The open and accepting approach for all those who require support created a mix of clients that would not usually be able to access traditional foodbanks. Helping working families that are in dire need, as well as the jobless and the homeless, is core to the way in which this non-traditional service was delivered:

> *"There will always be poor people, people with problems. There never seems to be a solution, just a reclassification of what poor is. About half the people that our foodbank provided for probably were not classified as poor or below the poverty line. They were normal working families that no-one knew about".*

The general purpose of this foodbank service was to provide families depending upon what they said they needed:

> *"So, if they said 'we are alright for cereal', we wouldn't give them that, but we would give fresh bread, butter and milk to ensure that they could make meals. However, because it was based on discretion, we could also buy fresh food...we provide non-perishable items, plus fresh milk etc".*

> *"There are families where fathers leave, mothers are long-term sick and they can't buy food... [so on one particular occasion] fresh chicken, mince and vegetables, [were provided for the preparation of full meals [to] freeze, which was more cost-effective than just giving tins of beans. We explained [that this kind of provision was] a one-off".*

People sometimes fall through the support infrastructure simply because of their age. If they cannot live at home, they may become sofa surfers, hoping one day to find a place of their own to live. However, as a young person with no dependents they would be very low down the list for housing support. Even if they do subsequently get somewhere to live they often have nothing or very little to live on:

> "We were supporting one lad who had a dog and I didn't realise at first, but he was giving the dog his food and he was just eating cereal... when I realised I got a big bag of dry dog food, which is much better for the dog. That made me realise that we should be helping people with food for pets too. So, I then changed our Facebook page to say that we would also be grateful for pet food and we got boxes of stuff, dog food, dog treats".

Another young man who fell foul of the system also needed urgent assistance:

> "One young lad had nothing, his benefits had been stopped, so we decided to spend fifty pounds on fresh items and things like washing powder, washing up liquid, sponges, shampoo, and all the other stuff outside of the normal non-perishable items. We even got him food for his dog. We explained it was a one-off, he was happy".

While we would like to think that we are immune to the kinds of circumstances that are described here, we probably all personally know someone who could use a helping hand and such a situation occurred during the time of this project:

> "One of my friends went through a bad time-he lost his job, was diagnosed with depression, his Mum moved away so he was left alone in a house he couldn't afford to rent, he didn't want to worry his Dad. I told him to use the foodbank, but it was hard because of his pride, in the end he did use the foodbank, but only twice. He could have used it more and no-one would

*have questioned it, but he just wouldn't abuse the system".*

## The community

When the wider community began to hear the stories of help for their friends or family members, who previously may not have been considered in a category that required assistance, they wanted to support this non-traditional foodbank. Also, service-users donated things that they did not need:

> *"...they wanted to support us because they knew we had supported their family when they needed it. So, they were helping us in return...we even got support from a young person's football team, they did some fundraising for us at a school and collected loads of food".*

> *"[Also]... people in the community started donating other things, like clothes. A consensus started to build about giving things that you don't use and we gave them to other services who could make use of them".*

## Service problems

It would be inappropriate to present this brave and untraditional approach to foodbank services as if it were a panacea. As with all attempted innovations, there are unintended and unexpected consequences. While there are always concerns over funds and resources for charitable causes, there are also unhelpful behaviours which may arise when people are faced with extreme situations:

> *"...one weekend I received a text asking for further help. I explained that the foodbank didn't open over the weekend and... I had a distressing situation at home that I had to deal with. A picture was texted to me as a form of*

*emotional blackmail. So I explained that I work full-time, the foodbank is my volunteer work and that I would appreciate it if she did not send such text messages in the future. I also explained that she was still able to continue using the foodbank service, but she didn't want to do so".*

## The final client

Unfortunately, the support of one client with problems of alcohol misuse eventually sounded the death knell for this innovative foodbank project:

*"After a few months the managers at the children's nursery became the primary [destination] for people collecting [foodbank parcels]...I'd just ring and say 'there is a service-user arriving today between 2-3pm, there is a parcel near the door', and that worked well until one service-user turned up intoxicated, aggressive and abusive. Obviously, because it was a children's nursery (young vulnerable children) we had to stop providing the service... and just stop!"*

## Reflecting on practice

While there was obvious sadness that the openness applied in this innovative project may have in some way led to its ultimate downfall, there are still many positive factors which should be acknowledged. Firstly, considering the provision of help without proof of poverty:

*"Everyone who was using the service stopped when they no longer needed it, which is why we used our discretion. We thought they would not abuse the system and they didn't because they were too appreciative. Why would we want to chastise someone who is poor by asking them to prove how poor they are? They can just ask for help, you give them help and when they don't need it anymore, you don't need to supply it. And if in three months' time*

*they need help again they can contact you for help without fear. People*
*worry that the system will be abused, but why would you bother for a few*
*cans of value tuna and some value cereal? They are not profiteering!"*

Another innovative perspective, where discretion allowed more help than
would be permitted through a structured system, was for people who
needed support to stay solvent when a domestic crisis happened. This was
enacted in order to avoid the kind of domino-effect which can eventually
lead to long-term financial difficulties:

*"...I think it's good for an organisation to have discretionary measures. You*
*shouldn't be reduced to supplying a single person with only three days of*
*food when they know they won't get any benefits for fourteen days as that*
*just promotes criminality. Also, if there are two parents with a young family*
*and it's a week and a half until they get paid when the fridge blows up. They*
*shouldn't have to get a referral from a governing body to get food because*
*they have had to spend their food money on a new fridge".*

## The last days and the impact on the dedicated young man who started the project

Despite many of the difficulties that had to be overcome, there are many
reflections of the supportive nature of individuals and organisations:

*"When we were running the foodbank we'd have low stock and high stock*
*sometimes. Kelloggs directly donated cereal, I worked at a supermarket and*
*they gave coffee that would be out of date within three months but too*
*much for us to use, so I contacted other organisations that refused to take*
*me as a volunteer and donated it to them...everything we got and couldn't*
*use was redistributed. We even got selection boxes at Christmas and Easter*

*eggs for Easter".*

However, once the incident at the children's nursery occurred, and it became too difficult to manage the project without such crucial provision of a storage area that also provided support for food collections, sadly it was decided that the facility must come to an end.

*"... I had minimal involvement near the end. I picked up from drop-off points, did a few deliveries, everyone did their bit to keep things running. If we'd had a storage unit it could have continued".*

Although the project had to end, it was important to all those involved that any stock was passed on for good use elsewhere:

*"We ensured that all the stock was given to a social housing group for young people, some other foodbanks, and food distributors. It was all donated on the basis that we could refer any of our existing clients and they would be supported. Of course, some places stipulated terms such as three days supply and a maximum of three times within a six-month period. In the weeks following closure we still received phone calls and we referred people to the other services".*

And the person who had been giving up his own food to feed his dog was not forgotten:

*"When we were closing down I rang him and said 'how are you, have you got enough food?'. He said that he was ok because his benefits had been sorted out. So I asked if he would like the stuff for the dog and he was really grateful, so I took it round to him. He could have lied and taken food for himself as well, but no, he didn't even think of abusing the system".*

The person who started this alternative foodbank project spoke about his commitment to working in the charitable sector, and how he struggled to find a way of doing so through the mainstream:

*"Every time I applied for a job, I didn't really have the right qualifications. I had GCSEs and A levels, but they want you to have a degree in that sort of sector".*

He had experience of working with homelessness outreach projects and carried a wealth of practice knowledge:

*"...with our homeless outreach programme the need is generally for the same sort of food, drink, clothing, and we add on a specific theme each month, so it might be hygiene-razors, soap, deodorant, talc, women's hygiene products. Another month it will be socks. We go through a lot of socks, then clothing, or sleeping bags, we ask people what will be most useful. By talking to people we found out that there is no point doing spicy rice for people who live on the streets, they have poor dental hygiene and open wounds so they can't enjoy that kind of food. Also, no point giving out cans of drink because they are not resealable, so bottles of water or juice are more practical. We give out small food packages that can be used immediately or kept until later. At the end of the night we would say that we had more food parcels left and did anyone want them and they wouldn't want to take too much, they would say-give it to someone else. So if you explain that it's the end of the night and you are going home, but would like the rest of the food to get out there, then they say that they will give it out to other people and that there are some known places where food is left for people to access'. But you don't know this stuff until you speak to people in that position".*

Although he had a high level of commitment to helping others and obvious practice knowledge, he could not find a place for himself in the sector which impacted upon the direction of his own future:

> "I probably won't go back to foodbank volunteering, but I do homeless outreach every month so I'll continue to do that. Near the end the foodbank was practically self-sufficient. We'd get enough donations to provide for service users. We had a network of volunteers who were happy to stock the larder and prepare food parcels to go out. The nursery was already operating'. However, the unexpected incident at the nursery could not be tolerated and as such the project came to an end, but this did not go unnoticed and by the time the project closed completely other provision had begun to, at least in part, close the gap that would be left: 'Since then local churches in the area have set up Trussell Trust foodbanks, which I think is fantastic. But Trussell Trust charge a license fee and because you go to this faith-based organisation, you have to keep to their policies. But at least there is something now in the local area which is good".

## Review and next steps for this default

While the founder of this foodbank hoped its unconventional arrangements would help some of those who had been left outside the emergency food system, he had no delusions regarding the eradication of food poverty. His expectation was that:

> "...foodbanks will always be needed' and not just for people who are experiencing unemployment: 'You are working, you have a mortgage, the maximum mortgage because of the house prices. You have children and everyone lives from payday to payday. Unfortunately, the car breaks down, [you could] get a payday loan, but what if you already have one? There will

*always be times like this".* Comments also related how close this type of situation is to all of us, the realisation that there are very few people who would not feel the impact of losing even part of a regular income for even a short period of time, and if not ourselves then those that we know: *"There are probably one or two people that you went to High School with who will need the support of a foodbank at some time. If you go to a primary school and look at everyone in assembly, you could say that at least one of them will be homeless by the time they are 18. We should address these things more in education; payday loans, debit cards, paying rent, water rates, council tax, debt management. We all need to know about this stuff".* Also, while he had not wanted his particular foodbank project to be affiliated with any faith group or foodbank management network, there was acceptance of power in shared resources: *"In the future, I think the best method would be combined benefits system with the Job Centre which maybe incorporates the Trussell Trust or another foodbank organisation, and debt management people and Citizens Advice people. And you should be given all the information for food, rent, etc in a leaflet pack because you might not need it right away but maybe in two months' time. If everyone just worked together it would be much better. There could be a database of services that says this person needs food in this area and the place closest can drop off food so that it's more streamlined".*

The founder had an uncommon approach to foodbank services and after spending time looking for a secular foodbank, which could not be found, he decided to collaborate with others to open and manage a foodbank in his local area. He did not want to operate as part of the established systems because:

*"...they operate on referrals only. They also have rules about how much food they can give and how often. And...there could be people outside the benefit system who need one-off help, maybe food for one month".*

This individual who wished to help his community had definite ideas of how this should be achieved. Based on his knowledge of the local area, and services which were already available, he wanted to organise a direct foodbank service that was open Monday to Friday. He wanted to avoid prescribed rules about how much food to give and how to give it, often by working from his own discretion. The goal was to provide food, non-food items, and advice about other services to anyone who asked for support. Of specific concern was the referral system adhered to by other foodbanks. He believed that individuals outside the benefit system could slip through the net, or simply not feel that they could obtain help. Another point of particular concern was that the foodbank should have no religious affiliation. There were a number of problems when setting up the foodbank, but it was eventually opened and the informal approach was described as:

*"Things ran well. When people came to volunteer, I would just say we need people to do this, that's what is expected of you. Do you want to be part of the foodbank? It was a small team, we had a lot of discretion and we wanted to help people'.*

The independent nature of the foodbank is specifically noted:

*"We didn't really access much from other organisations; we tried to be self-sufficient and rely on donations from the community. But we did offer our services to other agencies. I understand why [some foodbank management*

*organisations] have policies, because not everyone can be strong-willed like*
*myself and tell people when they are taking the Mick".*

This suggests an individual who saw the importance of supporting those in
his community when he observed difficulties and suffering, but also
believed that his local knowledge and understanding of the specific
environment would provide useful expertise. However, he was not naive
in his understanding and voiced a view that promotes good management
of the available resources. In addition, he raised the issue of
confidentiality:

*"I was turning volunteers away because they knew people who were using*
*the service, and as much as you can say this is confidential you don't want*
*to see a family member of someone you know there. When it's a small area*
*it can be embarrassing. So any sort of user interaction would be done by*
*myself or very few volunteers".*

While this consideration is based on due concern regarding potential
awkwardness for the individuals using the foodbank, it places heavy
responsibilities on a few and bodes ill for the long-term potential of the
facility. This is supported by the view that the required work for the
foodbank is:

*'...labour intensive, collecting food, putting it in storage".*

However, there was good community support when stock was required:

*"When the foodbank was low on provision of certain things, hot dogs,*
*beans, tomatoes, pasta sauce, pasta, tea, coffee, milk, [there would be] an*
*influx of soup or biscuits... you should never say 'we've got enough biscuits'*

*you should just receive what you can, if you have extra you can always donate them to another charity or trade swaps with them"*. The founder of this foodbank thoroughly believed in everyone's capacity to help others, as he said: *"...I don't think you need any special training to care"*.

While this statement underpins his belief system he also realised that, to follow his commitment of working to help others, he would need some form of higher education qualifications. In order to succeed in following a professional path he decided to return to education and complete a university degree.

# CHAPTER 7

# CONCLUSION, DISCUSSION AND COMMENTS

This whole research excursion began when an opportunity arose for individual interviews to take place at foodbanks around the North-West of England. This was of great importance and interest because of a notable shift in our social landscape, placing social need at front and centre due to an increase in financial pressures that put many more people, than we ever would have expected, in the position of using emergency foodbank services. Important too, is how information can be collected about the experience of individuals, and this was a chance to engage well-informed volunteers in sharing their narratives. Also here is a snapshot in time of a service, which is increasingly under pressure, to deliver to a growing number of users, without strategic management teams in place, without defined training of all support staff or, indeed, any operational planning of sites which are fit for operational purposes. Emergency food provision was called for and a volunteer movement answered the call with little in the way of professional support. Yet this volunteer service has become a vital part of a network of social provision in our communities. As such, it was a valuable opportunity to gather individual stories which represent a period of time when we cannot know for sure how the service will or will not be required to progress and how much more can sensibly be expected.

Therefore, the opportunity to collect the valuable narratives of the volunteer staff was taken with much gratitude for their personal and honest representations.

These interviews were the important catalyst for thinking much more widely about the volunteers who give their time and goodwill and also those who take on management responsibilities for many important community-based projects. There are many differences and similarities that can be seen just below the surface of these foodbanks and their everyday practices. Then, of course, there is the range of detailed literature which already exists in relation to foodbanks and management, some of which supports that which is said by our respondents. But the narratives add more, each one gives us something from the context and a personal view, which can often be lost in report writing, boardroom discussions and committee meetings. However, these are the important information platforms that society adopts by default, and they may miss important themes which are only brought to light by storytelling.

At all times the words of the volunteer workforce have been uppermost here and their dedication in assisting those in need is at the heart of this story. Their individual narratives come together in this place to add to the substantial and growing narrative of community support, which fights adversity and austerity for the common good and for survival of all, upholding the notion that no-one should be left behind. Above all this is a celebration of that which is achieved everyday in foodbanks around the North of England, the United Kingdom, and the world by volunteer organisations and individuals alike. This service to others shows true determination to provide assistance and give service. Important though financial pledges have become, such work goes beyond money as an object, the component of volunteering creates an action in practice of which provides much more even than food. It impacts favourably in environments where individual help is given to each human being. But just as it is said that we "cannot live by bread alone" so the foodbank gives more than food, it brings humanity, such as art and science require balance in our culture. This care for fellow human beings brings to mind a reflection of such importance portrayed in the arts, as an encounter with an angel, through the words of James Henry Leigh Hunt (1784-1859):

*...Exceeding peace had made Ben Adhem bold,*

*And to the presence in the room he said 'What writest thou?' – The vision raised its head,*

*And with a look made of all sweet accord, Answered, 'The names of those who love the Lord.'*

*'And is mine one?', said Abou. 'Nay not so,' Replied the angel. Abou spoke more low,*

*But cheerly still; and said, 'I pray thee, then, Write me as one that loves his fellow men'.*

*The angel wrote, and vanished. The next night It came again with a great wakening light,*

*And showed the names whom love of God had blest, And lo! Ben Adem's name led all the rest.*

(Abou Ben Adhem. James Henry Leigh Hunt)

Here humanity is the key, and such was the belief of Robert Greenleaf and his view of management practice. He was looking for beauty in practice which could be of service to all. Some time ago in the nineteen seventies, which does not seem so long ago to those in middle age , but closer to ancient history for many of our young people today, Robert Greenleaf's retirement was at hand and became the beginning of his commitment to recording his many years of experience through the lens of a belief that management and leadership could be a very different form of practice. He wished to work towards the improvement of the everyday lived lives of those working for and with those that held any form of control. Control can have such harsh implications when not practiced for the service of others. Those both in control and under control must amount to the vast majority of people and, therefore, a prize worthy of substantial work. He firmly believed that the crux of the matter lay within the perspectives of management and leadership responsibility. He took on this question and answered it through his concept of servant leadership. This deep and dedicated consideration of how people must want to serve in order to be worthy leaders sparked debate and research which continues today. Servant leadership as a concept purposefully places the servant first and leadership second. It promotes stewardship and particular responsibility, for service is to be seen as a precious gift and the most important of all callings. For if you are truly able to serve others, your capabilities will know no bounds. But the willingness to serve must be a constant, not a fleeting gesture. If service appears to be an easy route, please think once more. In the form of a servant leader, a person must work side-by-side with those whom they lead and, worryingly for some, must be open to recognising that others are capable leaders too. They should be pleased to claim that others are surpassing even those who are providing guidance. Such recognition is joy to the true servant leader because this is that which should be both inspired and inspirational in the cycle of servant leadership practice. There should be no fear of seeing that those whom you have served have become servant leaders themselves, for this would be the heartfelt wish. To seek to mentor those who may truly surpass yourself is the solemn point of servant leadership, this would be the zenith of achievement. Sadly, the perceived power inherent in management and leadership in our society often dictates a very different mindset to that which is described in the work of Robert Greenleaf. Those providing leadership should want to serve in equal terms and any inner revolt against such practice is a timely reminder to us all that self-interest creates a façade that suggests the high value of some achievements that may be of little consequence in the greater scheme of things. Disguise of this kind can discourage engagement with thoughtful approaches to management and leadership and is of little credit or help to anyone.

In regard to the range of literature which denotes or relates to servant leadership, the strength of appreciation for the work of Robert Greenleaf is profound. The original understanding portrayed in Greenleaf's early work is importantly kept at the centre of further extensions. Authors who had the opportunity to know and work with Greenleaf are valiant in their due consideration of the original essays and further developments of the theme. There is a fundamental understanding which weaves through the work of many other authors whose appreciation of the concept is clear and, moreover, there is often a keenness to underline the importance of furthering progress in practice of the servant leadership approach. Perhaps most have at least some personal recollection, some more extreme than others, of bad or even appalling management and leadership practices that have impacted negatively upon their own lives or others who have been blighted by such incidents. This is something that many individuals will have in common and feel completely impotent when considering how to expose and bring to an end the indulgent behaviour of one who may be causing anguish for many and in so doing thwarting the development of servant leadership.

While similar approaches, such as transformational leadership, are named as close in kinship there is never any doubt that servant leadership goes beyond all other concepts by the engagement of oneself in knowing the inner servant that is said to exist in all. It engages the practical process of acting as servant to support others as individuals. The individual is never lost sight of and no-one is ever left behind. The concept can, at any time of reading, appear simplistic and naïve with contrary heroic and statesman-like requirements running in parallel, just as being both servant and leader in harmony suggests dysfunctional practice. But human beings are more than capable of balancing such extreme anomalies as love and hate. Furthermore, there is something more beyond the acceptance of such things, an understanding that some things are wrong and while they may remain and continue in present times, they will one day be recognised as ailing and of consequence in depleting the human spirit. As such, stoicism is the practice of many who live under the daily bad practice of managers and leaders that are not and do not wish to be of service to anyone. Sadly, this equates to an uncounted throng as they are stoic every day when they must:

"...meet with Triumph and Disaster, And treat those two imposters just the same..." (Kipling 1895).

As is true of many such circumstances borne by the proletariat, unreported bad management practice and the indifference of self-centred leadership is arguably seen to be of little significance and may even be rewarded. If greater consequence existed for poor management and leadership, servant leadership development and practice would perhaps have long ago infiltrated the wider community and championed in all for-profit and not-for-profit organisations and institutions. Greenleaf establishes that people are our greatest asset; industrial revolutions, social development, and technological advancement are all founded on the work and progress of human beings, yet the way those beings are managed and led is often simply left to chance and is of little consequence, which begs a question about the indolence of such indifference. It seems that only the outcomes are precious and not the toil which produces them. Such is the concentration on only being a leader, while the work and dedication of the servant is demoted and undervalued, but there is not one without the other in the type of leadership that is equally kind and relevant for all. However, the servant leadership concept is not a magic wand to be waved or an enchanted algorithm to be run. It is too important to be allowed to remain mythical, servant leadership is a sophisticated idea that must be put into action in an imperfect world in a way that is most advantageous for each context under the premise that the notion of service to others is kept at its heart. If it does not remain rooted to the energy of being a servant, the notion of a healthy and hopeful servant leadership will not find traction. At its core servant leadership is as simple as empathy and as difficult as – empathy!

The literature in the context of foodbanks brings to the surface much that is shocking in everyday life. The poverty and desperation of individuals and families, the harsh truths around continuing deprivation which is alive and prospering in wealthy nations, and the cruel reality of child hunger are all reported in tragic repetition. Though this sad state of affairs lives on, it is obvious that governments are not choosing to intervene in ways that allow the picture to significantly improve. But, at grassroots level, lives are being supported, families are given hope and individuals find solace through community projects that provide food and much, much, more. Many contribute through networked organisations such as the Trussell Trust and as individual volunteers both associated to organisations and working independently in the service of others. While research continues with the minutes of meetings being recorded and numerous reports being written, it is still the daily volunteering of individuals in foodbanks, soup kitchens, community day centres and elsewhere that quite literally feeds the hunger which exists in communities. Reportedly, there are high numbers of volunteers in many spheres, and while there is a range of very different contributions made by volunteers we should not forget that they may be regularly experiencing events and environments which impact upon their own health and wellbeing. That is not to say that the volunteers represented here had great personal concerns, they did not. In fact, any noted concerns were linked with worries that the physical health of some older volunteers may mean that there would be problems in keeping the foodbank running. The practice in their service to support others was always paramount in their stories. This should be a concern for society given the steep increase in the use of foodbanks. The recent times of austerity share a timeframe with the increase of foodbanks and much greater numbers requiring assistance, but the categories of users have expanded to include many who would not previously have been expected to knock on their doors. Emergency food provision has become part of the history of many family lives in far more circumstances than was previously the case. Increasingly, families that are struggling to manage on low pay (rather than no pay) are finding that they also cannot cope without emergency support. The United Kingdom is a relative newcomer to foodbanks as a service and while they are sorely needed, and the volunteers are glad to be of assistance, no-one within the boundaries of this research believed that this is a long-term answer to the problem of food insecurity in a first world country.

The narrative account of foodbank volunteers, which are represented here, are both interesting and thoughtful contributions to the wide-ranging debate around aspects of emergency food provision. While they would all wish that the circumstances were different and that foodbanks were a thing of the past, this is sadly not the case and their ongoing service to the community should be celebrated. However, it is more than evident in their responses that they hold in high esteem those who take on the management and leadership responsibilities that go beyond the daily service requirements of the foodbank. Many feel privileged to serve with those who manage and lead, but also see themselves as servants. That is, servants who keep a very important service running, but also work in service of all the volunteers; caring for each of the group as individuals, facilitating their personal growth as well as the sustainability of the foodbank. Volunteering has created mixed groups of individuals that have been brought together by one cause and while they act as a team, they are not forgotten as individuals. They are consulted upon the work they wish to engage with, they are updated on cases that have caused concern, and they are encouraged to be part of a much bigger conversation about continued development and progress of the service they support. Much of the individual care which is practiced between this large unpaid workforce and their managers, is also mirrored in the ways in which they support each other whether in relation to work or issues in their own lives. As such, the servant leadership approach flows through action and practice. Instances of people who were, at one time, forced into circumstances that brought them to the foodbank as service users and then later began to work as a service provider is both heartening and inspiring. It is a clear example of the way in which service to others encourages continuing service to others. Even those who come to the service for a small number of emergency food rations and do not need the food packages again, sometimes return to say hello, to converse with the volunteers over a cup of tea and update them on their improved circumstances. Other useful examples of servant leadership by osmosis is previous service users returning with any goods that they could not use from their food packages, and when in improved circumstances, the action of contributing some further goods to the foodbank to help others who are in greater need. Such contributions and forbearance, even when their own personal lives may only be fractionally better than before, shows deep concern in the service of others and potential beginnings in themselves as servant leaders.

The managers themselves, or those who have simply taken the responsibilities by default, are not given the title of servant leaders by the volunteer staff, but the foodbank managers are described in such terms that it is impossible not to attribute related points. They are defined by their unending support for both volunteer staff and service users; they are noted for having a deep concern for each individual and spending a considerable amount of time, going far beyond the remit of the foodbank service. A great deal of praise and respect is attributed to the work that they do on behalf of the community. They are admired not only for being good operational managers, but also for caring, keeping up morale, retaining contact with service users who may need additional help, updating the volunteers on particular cases where they may have specific concerns about vulnerable individuals. Also though, they are respected for their capabilities in reasonably managing difficult situations with those who may seek to abuse the resources of the foodbank community projects. The volunteers are secure in the knowledge that they will not be left alone to deal with such difficult occurrences, the managers see such issues as their domain. In addition, managers are praised for taking time to understand what existing skills and competencies each of the volunteers brings to the project, and how personal negotiation takes place between managers and volunteers about the work they would feel most comfortable engaging with on behalf of the foodbank. Also the development of individuals is supported through internal and external partnerships on occasion.

While there is some interest in further development, volunteers suggested that their managers do everything possible to support their further development and some were in discussion about ways in which it could be extended. The managers were always supportive in such matters and did all they could to create opportunities for the ongoing development of the volunteer staff. This determination to support resolutions regarding individual needs amongst service users and volunteers, the care and attention for each person in their own right, the communication style of support and negotiation, and the purposeful attention to the appropriate development of each person, all point to effective elements of the servant leadership approach. Volunteers also commended their managers for their detailed and up to date knowledge of information and contacts that were vital in everyday practice, which demonstrates that these managers are reflecting on their own appropriate development too in the service of others. They do not hold the title of servant leader, often they have no title at all, but they do embody the spirit of servant leadership in action.

As much as it can be seen that the volunteer staff and their managers are giving of their care and attention, their time, and much more, still they look outside of themselves to attribute further admiration and this goes to the "Great British Public" and all other contributors of food, goods, and any other form of support. While it might be expected that they would reflect significantly upon their own contribution to the community, this is not so. The tributes go to the companies that allow "Food drives" and other forms of food contribution, and the public contributors who are seen as heroic in their unending and unstinting support for those in need. The huge generosity of the public never ceases to amaze the volunteers and they describe attending the food drives, which are allowed in some large supermarkets, and how individuals and families give away items from their own food shopping or make extra purchases specifically for donation. There are many different organisations such as: supermarkets, food manufacturers, independent shops and other businesses, schools, hospitals and, of course, faith groups, which make significant contributions throughout the year. As important as these are, and they are endorsed as being so, it is the individual acts of kindness which impact exponentially on the perspectives of the volunteers. It is seen as community endorsement for the work which continues out of sight of many. Accepting food personally from a stranger with a wish for it to be handed on to yet another stranger is said to be quite emotional for some of the volunteers who are on hand to receive donations. It is a demonstration of care and attention for someone beyond your own reach, but for whom you still assume responsibility as belonging to the same larger society, it is a wish that no-one should go hungry and, indeed, that no-one should be left behind. Again, we see the roots of humanity stretching toward and beyond all of us as equal in potential for participation in service and leadership. The actions of these personal donors are seen as endorsement for the work in which the volunteers are engaged and in some way provides solace for volunteers who may sometimes feel physically, mentally and emotionally depleted by fighting a social ill which will not be defeated any time soon. Certainly, the continuing stream of public donations appears to provide more hope than much of the government research and committee reporting that does little to change the level of emergency help required in communities.

When moving beyond the personal contacts sometimes contained within the action of donating, there are a number of concerns about the difficulties that foodbanks, as organised groups, face if they are to continue for as long as they are needed in communities. As a service for the vulnerable in society, their end would create even more severe circumstances for those who are reliant upon them. Therefore, worries around operational difficulties include: funding, extending the present provision, long-term sustainability, governments encroaching on the service and creating unhelpful rules, and long-term health issues of volunteers. These are not just concerns of the managers, as collaborative groups the volunteers discuss their concerns and consider potential solutions in conjunction with any networks they are affiliated with and review possible future planning. Such engagement with the wider scope of future focused operations also suggests the practice of servant leadership within each person, as they all want to contribute to the wider discussion and enable progress where they can.

The future of foodbanks is a highly debated topic throughout, research, conferences, in government and through practice. Again, the concern around government intervention and the possibility of government-run foodbanks is regularly raised. On a daily basis, the volunteers hear the personal stories of how stringent and austere benefit rules have forced some families into greater poverty. As such they fear that any implementation of rules might prevent them from supporting those who require assistance and simply create another part of a state social system which does not work effectively for the service users. The clearly stated wish of foodbank volunteers is that everyone has the opportunity of fair work for fair pay, rather than the low pay gig economy which has blighted the lives of many individuals and families. They don't want foodbanks to be run by the government, they want to see communities where foodbanks are unnecessary. However, there are also some warnings that there may always be gaps in any system and the result often being people who are simply unable to fill in a form for themselves and, perhaps, also struggle with budgeting, cooking, and coping with other basic requirements. This is seen as good reason enough to make sure there is always somewhere to go where they can make human contact. It is noted that, for some, access to online information will never provide the answers they need.

Away from the fears of the centralised government control of foodbanks, which may make them ineffective, but in a world where foodbanks are still necessary, the volunteers would hope for the future of the foodbank to include; more welcoming and café-like drop-in areas that provide hot meals, opportunities for people to have choice of picking their own food items, integration of a number of additional support services which could comprise benefit advice, referrals to other agencies, home deliveries, food clubs, cooking and home budgeting classes. All of these ideas show great empathy for communities which need support to progress, prosper and build a resilient future for themselves from within. In addition, there is exclamation over regular events, such as school holidays, people moving to different areas, and other extreme personal occurrences including death of a family member, divorce, illness and/or disability which may push people over the edge and leave them unable to manage. Such events and occurrences may need financial support, and foodbank service providers often see how the system of benefit allocation is too slow and, as a consequence, people are forced to utilise foodbank services. This is a highly ineffective way for short term support to be delivered when the individuals involved are already dealing with personal crises. They would hope for a different route for these individuals within a suitable contact system.

The narratives from the volunteer staff at foodbanks provide multi-faceted responses to how they see the future. They recognise that much of the provision that is needed exists through state benefits but in practice, and through a great deal of experience, they know that more and more people are experiencing difficulties and state provision just is not enough. They note that many other services, in addition to their own, such as housing associations extending their level of help for tenants in the guise of money management and even sometimes buying out personal loans. Community centres are also known for their good work providing lunch clubs, activity clubs, youth clubs etc. But it is acknowledged that independent provision is patchwork at best and the level of support can depend upon where you live and your knowledge of the local area. There is talk of future foodbanks that are extended to provide an umbrella of services for social support but this, of course, arises in want of a welfare state that works appropriately and circumvents the need for such things as foodbanks. The circle is considered as vicious rather than virtuous. Meanwhile, our courageous servant leaders look outside of themselves and continue to do what they can in difficult circumstances and seek to constantly improve. However, there is evidence on a daily basis of the importance of the service. Gratitude is overwhelmingly obvious from service users, and particularly from one respondent who could claim experience of being on both sides of the foodbank provision. High appreciation was explained when noting that:

> *"...the foodbank opened the doors to a family and the most important components are the people".*

Some foodbank volunteers made note of their specific attempts to find a secular foodbank in which to volunteer. They were unable to find such a thing and so decided to volunteer at a foodbank that was connected with a local church, although they were not congregation members themselves. A minority of foodbanks are independent entities, but they are not as many in number as those that are affiliated with faith groups. As part of this research the outlier chapter reports on such an independent foodbank. It represents the personal mission of an individual who wanted to serve the community but did not feel comfortable in doing so through a faith-based group. It details his initial journey to find a secular foodbank and his continuing journey that led him to support the opening of a foodbank based on his own principles and, sadly, the closure of the enterprise when it could no longer be safely managed within the community. Compassion for others specifically relates to the concept of servant leadership in practice, even the lack of a vehicle that embodied personal principles did not deter this respondent from delivering a foodbank service in the way in which he believed to be appropriate. His experience of volunteering to aid homeless people via outreach programmes, and his work in other foodbanks, led him to collaborating in the setting up of what he considered to be a secular foodbank. There were many hurdles that would have thwarted a less dedicated individual, but his determination to serve the community strengthened his resolve. For a time the service was available and helped a number of individuals, it also offered supplies to other providers. Some operational aspects were different from those expected in other more traditional foodbanks, for instance: people would self-refer, there were home deliveries, fresh produce was part of the service, bespoke leaflets on debt advice and benefit claims, among other issues, were included with the deliveries, and pet food was made available for people who had domestic animals in their homes. Support also came from the surrounding community in the form of volunteers, food and financial donations, offers of storage space, etc. This interestingly untraditional and innovative approach, which owes much of its practice to a youthful perspective of digital communication and pop-up business ideas, could not continue due to a very traditional issue of disruption that can only be averted or managed by having an onsite human presence. But if the traditional foodbank model is to adapt to the different ways in which people live in our modern society, useful lessons may be learnt from these potentially diverse approaches. Even though this foodbank operation included some alternative ways of providing the service, still the respondent could reflect on the future of foodbanks and how they may develop to be of even greater use. His main idea was a picture of the state system that included networked foodbank organisations (such as the Trussell Trust); debt management, information for everyone about all the types of services that they may need immediately or sometime in the future, and a database of services that alerts foodbanks to people in their area that need a delivery of food. While this respondent also would hope for a time when foodbanks are simply no longer required, his belief is that there will always be someone that requires additional help.

From all the commentary of the volunteers themselves, it is clear that they all agree that some form of safety net will always be required in societies such as ours. However, the net must be strong because when holes appear in the system, people fall through, lives are ruined, and families are left in desperate circumstances. Charitable organisations do what they can, and we are glad of it, but they cannot do all that is required when we are in times of severe austerity. Volunteering is a high-value activity, which should be cherished and not used as an excuse for avoiding the awarding of appropriate pay for worked hours. It should not be taken for granted that volunteers and volunteering will remain the same, many of these groups are well-informed, aware of political machinations, and critically consider the environment in which they serve. At a recent conference event in Manchester, one comment thrown across the room from an audience member was "should volunteers go on strike"? Perhaps this is what the environment of austerity has brought us to, the history of those groups that rarely strike and only do so under extreme circumstances are known to us, but sometimes desperation drives even those individuals to do something out of the ordinary. This would be a difficult decision indeed for those engaged in volunteering. It is an interesting idea to attempt impacting in the larger scheme of ongoing debate and argument. From the individual perspective no-one wants to see a closed sign hanging on the door of the foodbank, but such services do need to be taken seriously, rather than taken for granted. The volunteers, the managers and the servant leadership fortitude within them keeps the doors open for now.

# Summary

This study has provided an opportunity for the stories of foodbank volunteers to be expressed in their own words. The powerful narratives speak of much that is worrying when reflected upon from the perspective of a developed nation, and the overriding theme is that of a sad acceptance that foodbanks will not be consigned to our history anytime soon. While some volunteers suggest approaches to making foodbanks more acceptable, others are dismayed that they are required at all but also fear government takeovers that may reduce the service to just one more part of a larger system which is seeming to fail for many of those in desperate need of basic assistance. While all the volunteers are happy to be able to help, they would much prefer a system that does not require foodbank services. The existence of foodbanks is not as a cherished institution, but a sad reality of our modern-day western world. One particular message which surfaces from all the narratives is one of a social service system that just is not working and has to change. However, alongside this, another theme which is common from all respondents is their commitment to continue supporting others and reaching beyond the limited responses of government departments. Key to the central support of the majority of foodbanks are local churches and their parishioners, but also those who do not connect with a specific religion, but nevertheless band together with likeminded individuals who simply wish to provide help for those in distress. The dedication of this quiet army of individual volunteers enables the continuation of support for those in dire need. Many of the reflections here outline concerns for the future of our social services, but also inform on the potential of this volunteer service to continue in its support of local communities.

## Discussion

With the continuing growth of foodbank use reported by the Trussell Trust and further existing levels of deprivation reported by other research and charities, there appears to be no end to a greater burden of support being placed on our charitable services. Whether or not such services can be maintained in their current operational state is debatable. Certainly, the experiences reported here suggest areas of weakness within the system and strong rationales for planning development of such operations. There are important practical reasons why these charities will continue, much of which comes out of the understanding that their communities are in need of support and should not be neglected. However, these volunteering organisations are keenly aware that there are implications of impact upon the bigger picture of social service support and government decisions. Volunteers are many in number, they have a voice, and the narratives noted here are just a small part of the much wider story. That extended story must include those who have some greater power in government provision. Disturbing domestic situations are regularly recounted to volunteers and are often said to be due to very late decisions around the eligibility of state benefit and changes in the benefit system; this will not be altered by augmentation of foodbank operations, much more has to happen in other quarters!

Meantime, there are some warning flags that come forward from the narratives regarding the care and attention of volunteers, one most particular is that of the physical health of volunteers. In addition, is their dependence upon one manager or group leader who often is noted as the one person that deals with the most difficult of situations and holds all the most important knowledge and contact information. While these individuals are highly appreciated and valued, in practice it is a dangerous position to be in for any service. If this very special person, for whatever reason, can no longer continue, what happens to the service? Arguably, this is where servant leadership can be the greatest of strengths. As a concept, servant leadership engages people in the care and attention of others and importantly, guidance. As such, the individual physical health issues of each volunteer would be recognised. Also the development of the individual will be encouraged, so that more than one person would have the knowledge, skills, and information which may at this point be embodied by only one. Volunteers would also be encouraged to work from both a servant and leader perspective, combining their own experiences and practicing to help others to do the same. The narratives depict that some points of servant leadership are already strongly felt in the volunteering communities of these foodbanks. However, this is not something that can be left to chance. Many good things may already be occurring, but if safeguarding and development are to continue and increase it must be through the awareness of those who are willing to be servant leaders, and take on more substantial roles, as others inevitably leave or retire from the service. Foodbanks are busy places dealing with a number of issues through their daily operations, but much is dealt with by reacting to emergencies, rather than through succession planning. In part, conscious and subconscious thoughts that foodbank services should not be in existence in our wealthy country, perhaps, holds back future planning. Further concerns of whether the short term good of support is damaging the long game of forcing governments to take full responsibility is also of note. But within communities, where neighbours are struggling to feed their children, philosophical reflection and political posturing seems immediately to be unimportant and people begin to work in the service of each other, for better or for worse, and often for both. As such the practice and discussion will go on, as it must.

## Comment-implications, limitations and areas for further research

The servant leadership theory, as a dedicated and complete theoretical model of servant leadership, has not been specifically reported here. Instead, is some of the literature which helps us to understand the origins via the creative and thoughtful approach of Robert Greenleaf. His concept of people at their very core being natural servants, which in turn makes them worthy leaders, is a magical and hopeful manifestation of a truly optimistic and positive idea. This is not to say that it is impractical, like all good things, the sound of it is simple and the practice is not. Dedication, determination, and the motivation of many will perhaps bring forward servant leadership in practice for many more. For those who are developed as servant leaders and keep service at their heart, it is unlikely to be stress-free and easy, but it will surely be rewarding. For those who are colleagues of servant leaders within the workplace, their pathway will be facilitated by the support and trust, interest and personal engagement, together with managers and leaders who are, and will always be, servants first. This must then lead to an emerging model of future practice. The term "best practice" is avoided here as previously noted are the words of Peter Senge

(2006, 256) when suggesting the relevance of prototyping perspectives above that which has already been done:

*"Benchmarking and studying best practice will not suffice – because the prototyping process does not involve just incremental changes in established ways of doing things, but radical new ideas and practices that together create a new way of managing".*

Therefore, any emerging model of servant leadership may support what has been previously seen as good or best practice, but should not deny that the prototyping approach to recognising another way of managing may leave such that is already known, way behind. The managerial implications of this may be the ongoing development of practice which is forever held to the core conceptual theme of a heart of service, which would surely be a relevant place to begin and end, and to begin again.

Dedication, determination and the motivation of many is noted here as a way of bringing forward servant leadership in practice. In a time when there is such great need of innovation in perspectives of value, it is incumbent upon us to ask those who define the measurement of the next generation of leaders and managers, for innovative and contemplative decision-making. We are living at a point in time when our universities are measured in part by the number of graduates who gain graduate jobs or enter graduate schemes. This is an attempt to gauge if the higher education experience will lead students into well-paid, high-performance professions, because this is what is seen to be of value. As we are, at this time, desperate for people to support organisations which are at very least working to help sustain a reasonable society and, at best, shaping a valuable society for future generations, is there not good reason for placing the value of such professional routes (either paid or unpaid) alongside and on par with this graduate measure? Universities would be proud to develop such managers and leaders of the future, a future which sees and measures value in more, much more, than pounds and pence.

## Limitations of this study

The work reported here is defined as a qualitative study and does not seek to provide statistical evidence beyond that which is presented from other research as part of the literature and to support a number of points throughout the book. The contribution here is to highlight the incredible narratives of the volunteer workers in community foodbanks. In this instance, the focus is the North-West of England and the scope could be widened. However, given some specifics which have emerged, even greater focus on management insights for foodbank operations would appear to be of value, and the servant leadership approach in particular warrants greater attention in this context. In addition, research into the potential innovations within the day to day operations of foodbanks would also be of worth, particularly given the opportunities that are highlighted by the experienced volunteers who spoke about the future of foodbanks.

The methodological approach here was the recording of the personal stories of volunteers through narrative. This qualitative interview technique gives voice to the experiences of individuals in a congenial environment and does not dictate the direction or flow of the imparted information. Self-reflection is an important part of narration and allows thoughtful and rich stories of individual experience to come to the fore. A great degree of flexibility and thinking time is part of the narrative process. The narrative interviewer offers an interview environment which extends most of the control to the interviewee. However, there are a range of other methods which could be adopted to further this work, particularly if taken in a more prescribed direction, such as a focus on management and leadership practice.

For the purposes of analysis in this research, the constant comparison method allowed categories to be allocated based on the content of the narrative scripts and promoted organisation of the main points. Again, different methods of analysis could take this work in other directions if emergent themes were not utilised in this way. A short questionnaire was also utilised in this study, but only at the close of the individual stories when the narratives had reached a natural end. The questionnaire was a simple supporting method to aid the recognition of some demographic details (age, gender, education level) and some common themes from previous literature in the field. This may be seen as limiting and the questionnaire aspect of this research could certainly be extended.

As it stands, the research decisions made at the start of this work could now be viewed as limitations, and plans for further development of this work, or parts of it, may occur. However, of highest importance are the freely communicated narratives of the volunteers who kindly engaged with this project. The donation of their time and significant narratives are gratefully acknowledged. The heart of this study are the rich, penetrating and honest commentaries of the volunteering experience in the context of foodbanks. The gratitude of those whom they serve is evident, the duplication of goodwill is seen by return in the behaviour even of those that have little, wanting to donate whatever they can, but highest thanks indeed must go to all the volunteers who continue to arrive at the foodbanks, the street food projects, the community kitchens, and all the other places that provide nourishment, hope and much, much more. They are committed to the service of their communities and are proof in action that servant leadership exists and could not be more necessary than right now. What they do is not easy, long-term commitment can be hard, daily details of hardship and poverty leave their mark, and the longing to always do more is exhausting, but still they do this work. They find reasons to continue when it may be far easier to give in and give up, but they do not. As Kipling would have it:

*If you can force your heart and nerve and sinew*
*To serve your turn long after they are gone,*
*And so hold on when there is nothing in you*
*Except the Will which says to them: 'Hold on!'*

(If, Rudyard Kipling 1895)

Our volunteers hold on to those in need, they draw them close and help them through some of the worst of times, in places where many would not have expected to find themselves, and in a time when we must all acknowledge that the majority of people may be just one paycheque away from financial disaster. What precarious lives we lead! Welcome to the foodbank!

# Final Reflection on Servant Leadership

What is it that might be said about servant leadership as a twenty-first century approach to management and leadership? Firstly, for all those who have experience of being "managed", the reading of this concept gives hope that there may be a more useful way forward. Many are able to testify that substandard or inappropriate management is alive and thriving, as discussions with union representatives will attest. Poor management and leadership practice impacting upon our productivity is probably underestimated, which is interesting in itself given our modern-day obsession with productivity targets. Given that some of the ongoing unhealthy management and leadership trends (as evidenced by research and news reporting) the servant leadership approach provides an opportunity to reboot these important professional positions from grassroots level. Servant leadership is based on supporting the individual, serving the purpose of their individual progress, doing all that is possible through guidance, but this is a two-way street where all are servants and all should try to engage with their own leadership potential in the certain knowledge that it is the servant perspective that is at the heart of this approach. Appropriate leadership cannot occur without the servant at its core, which is by far the most difficult and most essential commitment. There is no leadership without service to others and service is the foundation and the essence of the concept. For an action of such importance, the measure of difficulty is of little or no consequence as enacting and inculcating service to others simply should be done.

Secondly, the idea of a person who is both willing and able to support and guide you in the pursuance of enabling you as an individual, is such a powerful narrative that it is difficult to argue against or even to find disagreeable. That is not to say that the guidance will always be what is expected and there are likely to be elements of discussion and potential misunderstandings, but all this is in the rationale of helping you, which is such a precious gift. For many, surely this is priceless indeed, even the dedication of time for discussion about oneself and one's progress (for the benefit of oneself alone) is a practice not usual in our time, if it ever was!

Thirdly, enabling service and promoting servant leadership holds the promise of riches. Some goodwill comes of this, for the individual there is the opportunity to grow within oneself and to extend this towards the service of others and potentially as a servant leader on a grander scale, but the two-way street must take effect, we accept the service of others in the same breath as committing to the service of others. It must be reciprocal if the concept is to gain a stronger presence. In this collaborative support mechanism, individuals become groups, groups become communities, and society has a paradigm worth perpetuating. Respect and support for other individuals is both right and proper as they have intrinsic value. The term "human resource" was not devised in order to undervalue human beings, but in the quest to quantify all of life we have undermined the individual human being as an entity and reduced it to a resource in many ways. This naturally happens in the English language because an item of resource is neither male nor female, it is a thing, an "it". Thereby being less important than something that is real with a personality and feelings. The "it" resource has a timespan of use while the he and she, the him and her, have lifetimes. They have independent lives and relationships, and decisions to make over the use of this time they might share with others. This can be a little or a lot, it can be effective and productive or not. Limited personal progress and development traps some into retrograde mindsets, while others are nurtured towards fulfilling lives. It is not difficult to imagine which route most of us would wish for ourselves, for others, and for our communities.

The most advantageous of possibilities must surely be the opportunities portrayed by Robert Greenleaf's servant leadership. While it is not said to be easy for those adopting this approach, and the approach is not said to be perfect, it is a way forward which promises potential benefits for all. A natural affiliation will exist for those who wish to support others and, in turn, may benefit from support. In short, servant leadership is the cycle of respect and understanding in the improvement of individuals, communities and organisations. This is the compassionate way to progress. It is sadly not the case that all managers and leaders are much interested in compassion that is, of course, until they are of want of it themselves. Then the lucky ones will find that there has been a servant close by and unnoticed all this time.

# REFERENCES

Adair, John. 2002. *Inspiring leadership: learning from great leaders.* London: Thorogood Publishing

AgeUK. 2014. *Age UK inquiry submission. APPG on Hunger and Food Poverty Inquiry.* https://www.ageuk.org.uk/globalassets/age-uk/documents/reports-and-publications/consultation-responses-and-submissions/equality-and-human-rights/appg_food_hunger_response_june_2014.pdf

AgeUK. 2015. *Evidence submission–Age UK evidence to the Work and Pensions Committee's Inquiry into* Benefit Delivery. https://www.ageuk.org.uk/globalassets/age-uk/documents/reports-and-publications/consultation-responses-and-submissions/money-matters/crs_sept15_age_uk_submission_to_work_and_pensions_committee_inquiry_on_benefit_delivery.pdf

AgeUK. 2016. *Working later, waiting longer. The impact of rising State Pension age.* https://www.ageuk.org.uk/globalassets/age-uk/documents/reports-and-publications/reports-and-briefings/money-matters/rb_nov16_report_state_pension_age_report_working_later_waiting_longer.pdf

All-Party Parliamentary Inquiry into Hunger in the United Kingdom. 2014. *A strategy for zero hunger in England, Wales, Scotland and Northern Ireland.* https://foodpovertyinquiry.files.wordpress.com/2014/12/food-poverty-feeding-britain-final.pdf

Barnardo's. 2013. *Families in need of food parcels – the food poverty crisis unwrapped.* https://www.barnardos.org.uk/what_we_do/policy_research_unit/research_and_publications/families-in-need-of-food-parcels/publication-view.jsp?pid=PUB-2220

Barnardo's. 2015. *Feeling the pinch: the impact of benefit changes on families and young people.*
https://www.barnardos.org.uk/feeling_the_pinch_2015.pdf

Barnardo's. 2015. *Briefing for Members Debate on Universal Children's Day in the name of Rod Campbell MSP.*
https://www.barnardos.org.uk/briefing_members_debate_universal_chil drens_day.pdf

Bogdan, Robert, and Sari Knopp Biklen. 1982. *Qualitative research for education: An introduction to theory and methods.* Boston, MA: Allyn and Bacon.

Breslin, Edward. 2017. *'Servant Leadership and Volunteerism'* In *Servant Leadership and Followership – Examining the Impact on Workplace Behaviour,* edited by Crystal J Davis, 1-24. Cham, Switzerland: Palgrave Macmillan, Springer eBooks

Bull, David, and Ellen Harries. 2013, *Beyond Beans: Foodbanks in the UK, New Philanthropy Capital.* https://www.thinknpc.org/resource-hub/beyond-beans-food-banks-in-the-uk/

Charity Commission for Northern Ireland. 2013. *Key lessons in charity governance-A thematic report,* Charity Commission for Northern Ireland

Church of England. 2019. *Church of England at a glance.*
https://www.churchofengland.org/more/media-centre/church-england-glance

Cooper, Niall, and Sarah Dumpleton. 2013. *Walking the breadline – the scandal of food poverty in 21$^{st}$ century Britain.* Church Action Poverty & Oxfam. https://www.scribd.com/document/340781627/Walking-the-Breadline-The-scandal-of-food-poverty-in-21st-century-Britain#download

Cooper, Kate. 2015. *Effective leaders create a culture of service.* Dialogue Review http://dialoguereview.com/effective-leaders-create-culture-service/

Covey, Stephen.R. 2016. *The seven habits of highly effective people.* Mango Media

Crowther, Steven. 2018. *Biblical Servant Leadership – An Exploration of Leadership for the Contemporary Context*. New York: Palgrave Macmillan, Springer eBooks

Davis Smith, Justin, and Pat Gray. 2005. *Volunteering in Retirement*. Joseph Rowntree Foundation. https://www.jrf.org.uk/report/volunteering-retirement

Department for Digital, Culture, Media & Sport. 2017. *Community Life Survey 2016-2017*. https://assets.publishing.service.gov.uk/government/uploads/system/upl oads/attachment_data/file/638534/Community_Life_Survey_-_Statistical_Release_2016-17_FINAL_v.2.pdf

Department for Environment, Food and Rural Affairs. 2014. *Household Food Security in the UK: A Review of Food Aid*. https://assets.publishing.service.gov.uk/government/uploads/system/upl oads/attachment_data/file/283071/household-food-security-uk-140219.pdf

Downing, Emma, and Steven Kennedy, Mike Fell. (Authors). *Foodbanks and Food Poverty*. 9th April 2014. House of Commons Library (SN06657). http://researchbriefings.parliament.uk/ResearchBriefing/Summary/SN06 657#fullreport

End Hunger UK. 2019. *Campaign win! UK government agrees to measure household food insecurity*. http://endhungeruk.org/campaign-win-uk-government-agrees-to-measure-household-food-insecurity/

European Food Bank Federation. 2019. *Mission*. https://www.eurofoodbank.org/en/mission-vision-values

Fabian Society. 2015. *Hungry for Change*. http://www.fabians.org.uk/publications/hungry-for-change/

Ferch, Shann Ray. 2011. *Forgiveness and Power in the Age of Atrocity: Servant Leadership as a Way of Life*. Maryland, USA: Lexington Books.

Finkelstein, Marcia. A, Louis. A. Penner, and Michael Brannick. 2005. *Motive, Role Identity, and Prosocial Personality as Predictors of Volunteer Activity*. Social Behavior and Personality 33(4) 403-418

Flick, Uwe. 2006. *An introduction to qualitative research* (3rd ed.). London: Sage Publications.

Frick, Don. M. 2004. *Robert. K. Greenleaf, A life of servant leadership*. California, USA: Berrett-Koehler Publishers, Inc.

Gentilini, Ugo. 2013. *Banking on Food: The State of Foodbanks in High-income Countries*, IDS Working Paper 415, Institute of Development Studies. https://www.ids.ac.uk/publications/banking-on-food-the-state-of-food-banks-in-high-income-countries/

Global Food Banking Network. 2019. *What we do*. Food Bank Leadership Institute. https://www.foodbanking.org/what-we-do/fbli/

Greenleaf Centre for Servant Leadership. 2019. *Greenleaf's Best Test* https://www.greenleaf.org/best-test/

Greenleaf, Robert.K. 2002. *Servant Leadership* [25th Anniversary Edition] A Journey into the Nature of Legitimate Power and Greatness. New Jersey, USA: Paulist Press

Hakanen, Jari.J, and Anne.B. Pessi. 2018. *'Practising Compassionate Leadership and Building Spirals of Inspiration in Business and in Public Sector'* In *Practicing Servant Leadership: Developments in Implementation*, edited by Dirk van Dierendonck and Kathleen Patterson, 119-140. Switzerland: Palgrave Macmillan

Harju, Lotta.K, and Wilmar. B. Schaufeil, Jari. J. Hakanen. 2018. *A multilevel study on servant leadership, job boredom and job crafting.* Journal of Managerial Psychology 33(1) 2-14

Harkins, Debra, and Kathryn Kozak, Sukanya Ray. 2018. Service Learning: A case of student outcomes. Journal of Service-Learning in Higher Education 8

Hill, Sonya.D. 2012. *Encyclopedia of Management 7th ed.* Servant Leadership. Detroit, USA: Cengage Gale p.897-899

Horsman, John.H. 2018. *Servant-Leaders in Training: Foundations of the Philosophy of Servant Leadership.* Cham, Switzerland: Palgrave Macmillan, Springer eBooks.

IFAN-Independent Food Aid Network-UK. 2016. *Volunteers across the UK giving 'at least £30 million' a year in unpaid work to support foodbanks.* http://www.foodaidnetwork.org.uk/food-bank-volunteer-hours

Indices of Deprivation Report. 2015. *Analysis for Manchester* (2015/v1.1).

file:///C:/Users/sckan/AppData/Local/Packages/Microsoft.MicrosoftEdge_8wekyb3d8bbwe/TempState/Downloads/F1_IMD_2015_summary%20(1).pdf

Institute of Leadership and Management. 2019. Trust in Leaders 2018. https://www.institutelm.com/resourceLibrary/trust-2018.html?utm_source=Institute%20of%20Leadership%20Management&utm_medium=email&utm_campaign=10593383_Trust%20Report%20and%20Resources&utm_content=Trust%20Report&dm_i=24KX,6B1WN,S5BQEO,OWMGC,1

Irving, Justin.A. 2018. *'Leader Purposefulness and Servant Leadership'* In *Practicing Servant Leadership*, edited by Dirk van Dierendonck and Kathleen Patterson, 25-42. Switzerland: Palgrave Macmillan

Joseph Rowntree Foundation. 2019. We cannot allow Brexit to distract from families locked in working poverty in our country. https://www.jrf.org.uk/press/we-cannot-allow-brexit-distract-families-locked-working-poverty-our-country

Kantharia, Bharat. 2012. Servant Leadership: An Imperative Leadership Style for Leader Managers. SSSRN E-Journal. https://www.researchgate.net/publication/228136358_Servant_Leadership_An_Imperative_Leadership_Style_for_Leader_Managers

Kipling, Rudyard. 1895. 'If' in *Rewards and Fairies.* https://en.wikipedia.org/wiki/If—

Lambie-Mumford, Hannah. 2013. *Every Town Should Have One: Emergency Food Banking in the UK.* Journal of Social Policy 42(1) 73-89

Lapointe, Emilie, and Christian Vandenberghe. 2018. Examination of the Relationships Between Servant Leadership, Organisational Commitment, and Voice and Antisocial Behaviors. Journal of Business Ethics 148(1) 99-115

Laub, James. 2018. *Leveraging the Power of Servant Leadership – Building High Performance Organisations*. Switzerland: Palgrave Macmillan, Springer eBooks.

Leigh Hunt, James H. 1834. *'Abou Ben Adhem'* In *The Amulet*, edited by S.C. Hall. https://www.poetryfoundation.org/poems/44433/abou-ben-adhem

Liden, Robert.C, Sandy J. Wayne, Hao Zhao, and David Henderson. 2008. *Servant leadership: Development of a multidimensional measure and multi-level assessment*. The Leadership Quarterly 19(2) 161-177

Liu, Helena. 2019. *Just the Servant: An Intersectional Critique of Servant Leadership*. Journal of Business Ethics 156(4), 1099-1112

Loopstra, Rachel, Aaron Reeves, David Taylor-Robinson, Ben Barr, Martin McKee, and David Stuckler. 2015. *Austerity, sanctions, and the rise of food banks in the UK. British Medical Journal*. https://www.bmj.com/content/350/bmj.h1775

Lu, Justing, Zhe Zhang, and Ming Jia. 2018. *Does Servant Leadership Affect Employees' Emotional Labor? A Social Information-Processing Perspective*. Journal of Business Ethics https://doi-org.salford.idm.oclc.org/10.1007/s10551-018-3816-3

Mason, Rowena, and Patrick Butler. 2014. *"DWP advising jobcentres on sending claimants to food banks"*. *The Guardian*, March 11, 2014 https://www.theguardian.com/society/2014/mar/11/food-bank-jobcentre-dwp-referrals-welfare

McEachern, Morven, Caroline Moraes, Andrea Gibbons, and Lisa Scullion. 2019. *Research brief: Understanding Food Poverty and the Transitional Behavior of Vulnerable Individuals*. Salford: University of Salford.

Moore McBride, Amanda, Jennifer C. Greenfield, Nancy Morrow-Howell, Yungsoo Lee, and Stacey McCrary. 2012. *Engaging Older Adult Volunteers in National Service*. Social Work Research 36(2) 101-112

National Council for Voluntary Organisations-UK. 2014. *How Many People Regularly Volunteer in the UK?* https://data.ncvo.org.uk/a/almanac14/how-many-people-regularly-volunteer-in-the-uk-3/

National Council for Voluntary Organisations-UK. 2019. *Policy and Research-Volunteering.* https://www.ncvo.org.uk/policy-and-research/volunteering-policy

Nesbit, Rebecca, Heather Rimes, Robert K. Christensen, and Jeffrey L. Brudney. 2016. *Inadvertent Volunteer Managers: Exploring Perceptions of Volunteer Managers' and Volunteers' Roles in the Public Workplace.* Review of Public Personnel Administration. 36(2) 164-187

Newman, Alexander, Gary Schwarz, Brian Cooper, and Sen Sendjaya. 2017. *How Servant Leadership Influences Organizational Citizenship Behavior: The Roles of LMX, Empowerment, and Proactive Personality.* Journal of Business Ethics 145(1) 49-62

Nichols, Joe. D. 2010. *Teachers as servant leaders.* Lanham: Rowman & Little field Publishers

Noyes, James, and Philip Blond. 2013. *Holistic Mission-Social action and the Church of England,* Resurgo/ResPublica

Nsiah, Joseph, and Keith Walker. 2013. *The Servant Leadership Role of Catholic High School Principals.* Rotterdam: Sense Publishers

Palmer, David. 2012. *Management Reporting Issues: One of a Series of Guides for Financial Management Development,* Charity Management No 701

Parris, Denise.L, and Jon W. Peachey. 2013. *A Systematic Literature Review of Servant Leadership Theory in Organisational Contexts.* Journal of Business Ethics 113(4) 377-393

Qiu, Shaoping, and Larry Dooley. 2019. *"Servant leadership: Development and validation of a multidimensional measure in the Chinese hospitality industry",* Leadership & Organization Development Journal, Vol. 40 Issue: 2, pp.193-212, https://doi.org/10.1108/LODJ-04-2018-0148

Roberts, Gary. 2015. *Developing Christian Servant Leadership-Faith-based Character Growth at Work*. USA: Palgrave Macmillan

Salamon, Lester.M, and Helmut K. Anheier. 1992. *In search of the non-profit sector. I: The question of definitions*. Voluntas: International Journal of Voluntary and Nonprofit Organizations 3(2) 125-151

Scheier, Ivan. 1996. *'Guerrilla Goodness-an interview with Ivan Scheier'*. In *In Context* (p. 27). The Context Institute, edited by E. Cooper and G. Cooper. http://www.context.org/iclib/ic37/scheier/

Shen, Huei-Wern, and Tam Perry. 2012. *Interdependence between the Social and Material Convoy: Links between Volunteering, Widowhood, and Housing Transitions*. Social Work Research 40(2) 71-82

Schwarz, Gary, Alexander Newman, Brian Cooper, and Nathan Eva. 2016. *Servant Leadership and Follower Job Performance: The Mediating Effect of Public Service Motivation*. Public Administration 94(4) 1025-1041

Scicluna Lehrke, Alyse, and Kristin Sowden. 2017. *'Servant Leadership and Gender'* In *Servant Leadership and Followership – Examining the Impact on Workplace Behaviour, edited by Crystal J Davis*, 25-50. Cham, Switzerland: Palgrave Macmillan, Springer eBooks

Second Harvest Foodbank. 2019. *The History of Foodbanking*. http://www.hungernwnc.org/about-us/history%20of%20food%20banking.html

Senge, Peter. M. 2006. *The Fifth Discipline – The Art & Practice of The Learning Organisation*. London: Random House Business Books

Shelter. 2016. *One in three working families only on paycheque away from losing their home*. https://england.shelter.org.uk/media/press_releases/articles/one_paycheque_away

Smith, Norman. 2010. *Analysis: David Cameron launches Tories' 'big society' plan*. https://www.bbc.co.uk/news/uk-10680062

Smith, Karen. 2012. *Exploring flying faculty teaching experiences: Motivations, challenges, and opportunities*. Studies in Higher Education, 39(1), 117–134.

Social Metrics Commission. 2018. Social Metrics Commission launches a new measure of UK poverty. http://socialmetricscommission.org.uk/social-metrics-commission-launches-a-new-measure-of-uk-poverty/

Spears, Larry.C. 1998. The Power of Servant Leadership. San Francisco, USA: Berrett-Koehler Publishers

Stephenson, Jacqueline.H. 2017. 'Leadership and Diversity in Management' In Servant Leadership and Followership – Examining the Impact on Workplace Behaviour, edited by Crystal J Davis, 81-108. Cham, Switzerland: Palgrave Macmillan, Springer eBooks

Sumi, Robert, and Dana Mesner-Andolsek. 2017. The integrity of the servant leader. Abingdon, Oxon: Routledge

Taylor, Anna, and Rachel Loopstra. 2016. Too Poor to Eat, Food insecurity in the UK. http://foodfoundation.org.uk/wpcontent/uploads/2016/07/FoodInsecuri tyBriefing-May-2016-FINAL.pdf

The Guardian. 2019. "Foodbanks are no solution to poverty". The Guardian. March 24, 2019 https://www.theguardian.com/society/2019/mar/24/food-banks-are-no-solution-to-poverty

Third Sector. 2018. The public view: charities do good work, but we don't like how some behave. Third Sector Magazine. https://www.thirdsector.co.uk/public-view-charities-good-work-dont-behave/communications/article/1493061

Trussell Trust. 2019. Volunteer with us. https://www.trusselltrust.org/get-involved/volunteer/

Trussell Trust. 2019. Foodbank statistics for previous financial years with regional breakdown. https://www.trusselltrust.org/news-and-blog/latest-stats/end-year-stats/

Trussell Trust. 2019. Latest Statistics 2013-2019. https://www.trusselltrust.org/news-and-blog/latest-stats/

Trussell Trust. 2019. *End of Year Stats.*
https://www.trusselltrust.org/news-and-blog/latest-stats/end-year-stats/

Trussell Trust. 2019. *More Than Food.*
https://www.trusselltrust.org/what-we-do/more-than-food/

UK Charities Commission. 1995. *Milestone-Managing key events in the life of a charity.*

https://www.gov.uk/government/uploads/system/uploads/attachment_
data/file/284726/rs6text.pdf

Veeder, Heather.L. 2011. *The connection between servant leadership and service learning in the context of higher education.* The International Journal of Servant Leadership 7(1) 177-190

Verdorfer, Armin.P, and Johannes Arendt. 2018. *'Mindfulness as a Building Block for Servant Leadership'* In *Practicing Servant Leadership,* edited by Dirk van Dierendonck and Kathleen Patterson Switzerland: Palgrave Macmillan

Volunteering Australia. 2016. Definition of Volunteering.
http://www.volunteeringaustralia.org/policy-and-best-
practise/definition-of-volunteering/

Wengraf, Tom. 2001. Qualitative research interviewing: Biographic narrative and semi-structured method. London: Sage Publications.

Wengraf, Tom. 2004. Boundaries and relationships in homelessness work: Lola, an agency manager. Forum: Qualitative social research.
http://www.qualitative-
research.net/index.php/fqs/article/view/658/1424

Whang, Zhen, Haoying XU, and Yukun Liu. 2017. *Servant leadership as a driver of employee service performance: Test of a trickle-down model and its boundary conditions.* Human Relations 71(9) 1179-1203

Wheeler, Daniel.W. 2012. *Servant Leadership for Higher Education –
Principles and Practices*. San Francisco: Jossey-Bass.
https://books.google.co.uk/books?hl=en&lr=&id=fPYBqOa6mtoC&oi=fnd
&pg=PT9&dq=servant+leadership+in+higher+education&ots=OomWmx8
4IR&sig=7P9iUvuB1b-qX7di7bsxcoMGmmM#v=onepage&q=servant%20
leadership%20in%20higher%20education&f=false

Whittington, J. Lee. 2018. *'Creating a Positive Organization Through
Servant Leadership'* In *Servant Leadership and Followership – Examining
the Impact on Workplace Behaviour*, edited by Crystal J Davis, 51-80.
Cham, Switzerland: Palgrave Macmillan, Springer eBooks

Winne, Mark. 2008. *Closing the Food Gap: Resetting the Table in the Land
of Plenty*. Boston, Massachusetts, USA: Beacon Press.

Yang Ziwei, Haina Zhang, Kwong Kwan, and Shouming Chen. 2018.
*Crossover Effects of Servant Leadership and Job Social Support on
Employee Spouses: The Mediating Role of Employee Organization-Based
Self-Esteem*. Journal of Business Ethics 147(3) 595-604